Tall Tales for Tired Times

T.T.T.T

David Lewis Paget

BARR BOOKS

For my Reviewer Friends
On WritersCafe, Poemhunter,
Poetfreak, Writers-network,
Apollo Blessed and Hello Poetry

Other Poetry available by the author:

Pen & Ink – The Complete Works 1968-2008
Timepieces – The Narrative Poetry
At Journey's End – The Narrative Poetry, Vol. II
The Demon Horse on the Carousel – and Other Gothic Delights
Poems of Myth & Scare
The Devil on the Tree – and other Poems of Dysfunction
Tales from the Magi
Taking Root
The storm & the Tall-Ship Pier
The Season of the Witch
Smugglers Pie
My China
The Book on the Topmost Shelf
The Red Knight

ISBN – 978-0-9807148-4-5

All Poems
Copyright © 2014
By David Lewis Paget

All Rights Reserved

Contents

Foreword 5

1. The Sacrifice and the Cloud	7
2. The Timeless Cave in the Cliff	9
3. The Glow on the Outback Hill	12
4. The Upstairs Witch	15
5. The Long Wait	17
6. The Conversion	19
7. Once all the Books are Gone!	21
8. Dance with the Devil	23
9. Distance Never Lies!	26
10. The Witch of Aberdare	29
11. Born for Raising Hell!	31
12. The Party Prank	33
13. On the Other Side of the Door	35
14. The Parchment Scroll	38
15. The Cast-Off	41
16. All Hallows Eve	43
17. Sister Switch	46
18. Dark Portents	48
19. The Isle of Gods	50
20. The Old Man in the Park	53
21. The Courtship of Sisters Three	55
22. The Attic Rats	58
23. Strange Pathways	61
24. The Buried Past	63
25. The Headland Wreck	66
26. Teaser	68
27. Following Jane	69
28. Trick or Treat	72
29. The Enchanted Manor	74
30. The Paper Girl	78

31. House!	80
32. The Secret Wood	82
33. Beside the River Wye	84
34. Family Secret	86
35. Deny, Deny!	89
36. The Basement Stair	91
37. Five Hundred and One	94
38. Man in the Future Past	97
39. Lady Jane	99
40. I Can Read Your Mind!	102
41. Talk is Cheap!	104
42. The Will of God	107
43. That Was Then…	108
44. Heaven, Hell or the Highway	110
45. Isle of the Dead	112
46. The Terror!	115
47. The Ruined Church	117
48. Midnight	119
49. The Gamekeeper	120
50. Goblin Castle	123
51. Stroke!	126
52. Our Parting Ways	128
53. Don't Come Here Anymore!	130
54. The Crone Who Lived in the Well	132
55. The Final Rest	135
56. A Christmas Tale	138
57. The Magnetic Girl	141
58. A Letter from Bedlam	145
59. The Misunderstanding	146
60. Crow Fly-Over Night	149
61. The Burial	150
62. Bells and Motley	152
63. Heart Stopper!	155
64. Zanzibar!	158

Foreword

Departing for once from my own tradition, which is to name each book after a prominent poem, which is then placed at the front, the title of this book has no such poem associated with it. Tall Tales for Tired Times is exactly what it says it is. We live in tired times. I can never remember a time when the world was in such a tumult of aggressive wars, famines, populations fleeing, religions clashing – though no doubt they have in the past. One only has to look back to the Inquisition to see what barbarous events may be provoked once intolerance of one or more religions boils over. We humans seem to be incapable of living in harmony with anyone who does not share our own religious views. The only one who seems to have no particular religion is God himself, though his name is taken in vain by every clique and breakaway church.

But no, the times are also tired on account of the overpopulation of the planet. Seven billion now, twelve billion within about thirty years. We will no longer be able to feed ourselves, and the thought of that makes me feel very tired indeed. So the stories in this slim volume have absolutely nothing to do with the real world. They are a means of escape, from reality, from despair, from the grind of daily living. They will transport you into my own imaginative universe, with its strange parameters of improbable situations in an alternative world that you may inhabit between these pages, and nowhere else. There is love, blood, gore and more, but once finished, you may comfortably fall asleep, secure in the knowledge that this world does not exist outside the boundaries of your own secret universe.

David Lewis Paget

December 2014

The Sacrifice and the Cloud

The cloud hung over the mountainside
Like a black and evil pall,
It took the sun from the valley, and
It held the folk in thrall,
The crops lay dormant in the fields
For they wouldn't ripen now,
The farmers down in the valley cried,
'It has to go, but how?'

They'd watched the cloud as it gathered
Bringing a dark and fierce storm,
With hail that battered the tender shoots
And flattened the barleycorn,
They shook their fists at the darkening sky
At this untoward attack,
But the cloud had threatened them, by and by
When the lightning answered back.

Then thunder rolled down the mountainside
And it shook their rustic homes,
It rattled the beams and the rafters, and
Was felt in their feeble bones,
They thought the wind would blow it away
But the air up there was calm,
And still it hovered there, day by day
To blanket each valley farm.

The tiny Kirk was amass with men
Who'd never been there before,
In hopes that a sudden show of faith
Would bring their god to the fore,

But the cloud still leered from the mountaintop
For weeks, and it hung there low,
'Perhaps the answer is not with God,
But the gods of long ago!'

The older men in the village thought
The answer might lie with Baal,
And some had prayed to the thunder god
But the answer they got was hail,
'There must be something the elders knew
To bring such things to a stop.'
'That cloud up there is the Wandering Jew
Who never may reap a crop.'

They racked their brains for the thing to do
And one of them wasn't nice,
'What we need is a virgin girl
To send up a sacrifice.'
So they seized a maid called Annabelle,
Whose parents were dead and gone,
And dragged her up to the mountaintop
In hopes it would move along.

But they weren't too sure just what to do,
Should they play a chord with a lyre,
Should they sound a note, then cut her throat
And throw her corpse on a fire?
She screamed at the top of her voice, just once
And the sun came shining through,
'I've not been a virgin now, six months,
But I wouldn't be telling you!'

The Timeless Cave in the Cliff

He found a little frequented cove
As he sailed the Southern Seas,
An island, not on a current map,
But one bereft of trees,
I only know, for he left a note
In that cave, way up in the cliff,
And it's had me wondering ever since
Not how, or why, but if?

What was left of his boat was there
Washed high, out there on the shore,
Battered and beaten by storm and tide
Ten years, or maybe more,
The Isle was barren and treeless, not
One thing would pleasure the eye,
Except the cave in the towering cliff
Well up in the face, and high.

I anchored there and I rowed ashore
Then I walked around to the face,
Somebody else had been there before,
A rope was still in place,
I'd never been much of a climber, but
I scaled that rope all right,
Just as the sun was going down
So I had to spend the night.

The face of the cave was sheltered, and
The weather, it wasn't cold,
I curled up deep in a corner 'til
The dark had entered my soul,

I dreamt of many a sailing ship
And men of a stately mien,
Who stalked grim-faced through a whirlpool race
In a land that I'd never seen.

And up above was a starlit sky
That had seemed to spin and curve,
Taking the glow of the Pole Star south
With the curvature of the earth,
I woke when the first few beams of dawn
Shone in from a blighted sea,
Where my boat had tugged at its moorings
In an effort to cast it free.

The cave led into a passageway
That was dimly lit in the dawn,
I ventured along it gingerly
Over moss, as green as lawn,
Then I came on a line of candles, set
In the rock to light the way,
Into the heart of a grotto there
Where a pool of water lay.

The pool was glowing an azure blue
From a light reflected below,
That shone back down from the ceiling rock
In a shifting, glittering show,
And beyond the pool was an altar there
That hadn't been made by man,
Of shining stars and a crescent moon
And a figure that looked like Pan.

I tip-toed cautiously round the edge
Of the pool til I came to stand

Right in front of the altar there,
Half covered with silt and sand,
And lying crouched at the side of it
Was a huddle of ancient bones,
That lone seafarer who'd left his yacht
And followed these stepping stones.

The bones lay there in a deep despair
As of one who'd given up hope,
He must have come with the boat out there
And climbed with that length of rope,
But the bones were grey, looked terribly old
Too old for that boat, it's true,
With the fingers gripping a note, half ripped,
The one that I'll read to you.

'You've come to an Isle where there is no time,
So take this note and be gone,
I came, like you, from out of the blue
When I woke, time travelled on.
The stars spin crazily every night
And they thrust me into the past,
I woke to find that my boat had gone
And the cove was covered in grass.'

'It could be a million years ago
It could be a future time,
The sea has receded, that I know
And the year, it isn't mine.
The altar glows with the crescent moon
When a major shift occurs,
And the devil man that looks like Pan,
I think that his seed is cursed.'

I took the note and I stumbled out
Of the cave, and slid the rope,
Then ran back over the beach, and rowed
Back out to my world, my boat.
I hadn't been more than an hour away
When the heavens went black, and weird,
I looked behind and I feared to find
The Island had disappeared!

The Glow on the Outback Hill

We hadn't had TV news for days
And the nights were cold and still,
The radio sound was just a haze
Of hash, from over the hill,
There wasn't a signal for the phone
And the Internet was dead,
'Do you think it's just the weather, Bill?'
'Much more than that,' I said.

The power went off on the seventh day
I began to feel alarm,
We'd never felt quite so isolated
On our outback farm.
I drove on out to the neighbour's spread
But they seemed to have gone away,
I thought, 'That's funny, it's not like Fred,
He's usually baling hay.'

I came back via the Rogers place,
There was nobody around,
The doors to the house were open, but
They seemed to have gone to ground.

Their cars were there but the truck was gone
And the old Toyota Ute,
I called and listened, but not a sound,
I should have been more astute.

I should have packed, and driven away
If I'd known what I know now,
But the pigs and the chickens had to be fed,
And what to do with the cow?
I couldn't think much outside the farm
The world could fend for itself,
We lived in a tiny world of our own
And thought about nothing else.

We lit the paraffin lamps at night,
'It's lucky we kept them, Bill.'
I said, 'You're right,' and stood on the porch,
And watched the glow on the hill.
We'd had three days of never a breeze
Like the lull before a storm,
Though the clouds glowed red in the sky at night
In shapes that were ripped and torn.

A rumble began the thirteenth day
Like a thundering from afar,
And Jacqueline turned to me to say,
'Stop leaving the door ajar!'
She then collapsed, and covered her ears
And bent down low in her chair,
I saw that her face was smeared with tears
And all I could do was stare.

'You know that I love you, Jacqueline,
Whatever may come to pass,

I love you more than the day before,
I just want to tell you, lass.'
It started raining at just on dusk,
Came down, and started to pour,
It raised a mist, and started to hiss
In the barley stooks by the door.

The lightning started at four a.m.
We hadn't been able to sleep,
The sky ablaze through a purple haze
I could hear my woman weep.
I wiped the dust off the .22
That I'd kept there, under the stairs,
Loaded a fresh new magazine
And silently said my prayers.

The cow was dead in the morning, lay
Quite burned, and covered in blood,
And all the chickens were strewn about
Quite dead, they lay in the mud,
'What does it mean,' said Jacqueline
As she stared through the window pane,
'I don't want to be too hasty, love,
But I think it was acid rain.'

'There's nobody left but us,' she said,
Be honest and tell me true!'
'I don't want to jump to conclusions, but
There's something we need to do.
Pack up our clothes, and all the food,
We'd better be heading West,
If Sydney's gone, a hydrogen bomb,
Then Melbourne would have been next.'

We're headed on out to who knows where
And leaving the rain behind,
I hope that the cloud won't follow us there
Though we'll be travelling blind.
The .22 is behind the seat
In case we have need of it,
I pray to God that we'll have it beat,
But Jacqueline's just been sick!

The Upstairs Witch

I woke to a knock at the door one day,
And stumbled, to put on my gown,
The place was a shambles, and last night's tea
In cartons, was scattered around.
I hate people seeing the way I live,
They shouldn't call round, it's a bitch,
But called out, 'Who is it?' and got the reply,
'It's me, it's the upstairs witch.'

I had no idea she lived upstairs,
The apartments are all very small,
The slightest of noises will carry on through
The ceilings, and paper thin walls.
I opened the door in bemusement then
To see who was pulling my leg,
She wore every colour the rainbow sent,
Pushed past me, and said: 'Call me Peg!'

I followed her into the wreck of my room,
And mumbled, 'I know, it's a mess.'
She shrugged, and she pointed my PC out,
'I knew it was that, nothing less!

You sit and you type through the early hours
I hear all your whistles and bells,
Your tappity-tapping is driving me spare,
And worse, is confusing my spells.'

'I have to compose when the mood is high,
And that is from midnight and on.'
'And I only spell when the Moon is nigh,
I can't til the sun has gone.'
We stared at each other with little grace,
Both grim, with a certain intent,
She wouldn't be giving an inch to me,
I murmured I wouldn't relent.

'We'll have to come up with a compromise,
I'll help you, if that helps myself,
I'll spell in your program a silence key,
And you'll be at peace with yourself.'
'But what am I getting from you in return,
This sounds like it's going one way…'
'I'll bring all your stories to life,' she said,
'In colour, and one for each day.'

'I've written so many, you'll never keep up,
I'll need to go back through my files.'
'Just open the drawer of your cabinet,
And I'll carry you there, for a while.
I've seen all your stuff on the Internet,
Your devils and demons and ghouls,
I haven't a clue what you think you will do
In a garden, with so many fools.'

She sits in her garret and plays with her spells,
I type without making a sound,

I open the drawer and I walk on the shore
Or hear bells from the church in the town.
I follow each lady I've written in verse
And make love when I'm feeling the itch,
They all wear the colours of rainbows at first,
And they look like the upstairs witch!

The Long Wait

She sat and stared from the window ledge,
She sat and stared at the sea,
Was sitting all through my childhood there
Since Eighteen fifty-three,
They said that she'd only stand upright
When a sail came into the bay,
When a ship came back from the Indies, or
Returned from Mandalay.

Nobody knew what she did in there,
She knitted, or she sewed,
Perhaps she was sat embroidering
As she watched the old sailroad,
They say she looked for a purple sail
Run up at the mizzen mast,
A sign that a certain Captain Hale
Had sailed on home at last.

She had a gentle and kindly face
I remembered from my youth,
But time went on and her face had shone
With tears, to tell the truth,
Her beauty gradually faded as
The years, they took their toll,

And sadness leached from her pale blue eyes
Before the house was sold.

A ship sailed into the harbour on
A warm spring afternoon,
A tattered sail at the mizzen that
Had lost its purple bloom,
The Captain wandered along the shore
From out where the sea was calm,
And stopped to gaze at a window,
But with a brunette on his arm.

He shook his head for a moment
As at a distant memory,
One of a thousand left behind
In the years that he'd spent at sea,
His eyes were held for a moment by
The eyes at the window pane,
But then he turned to the young brunette,
And went on his way again.

I bought the house when the sign went up
Though the agent said, 'You're sick!
I wouldn't be touching that tumbledown,
It's just a pile of brick.
Nobody's been in there for years,
The thing needs pulling down,
You'll get the place for a song, of course,
But there's better in the town.'

I went and I picked the key up and
I stood out on the grass,
And stared on up at the window that
Was crazed, with broken glass,

The house was dark as a midden, all
Was shrouded in a gloom,
I felt my way up the passageway
And ventured in that room.

She sat quite still with her back to me
And stared out as before,
The window, it was crazed and cracked
And that was the most she saw,
I walked up slowly behind her, though
I didn't know what to say,
She looked as if she'd been porcelain,
But now she was only clay.

I had the glazier fix the pane
And I locked that room up tight,
I wouldn't let anyone go in there,
It didn't seem to be right.
I put on a Captain's hat, and stand
Between the house and the sea,
And swear that I see a gentle smile,
But now, she's looking at me!

The Conversion

She'd come down alone from the house on the hill,
But changed, I could see that too,
'I can't, any longer, keep seeing you Phil,
I just don't believe in you!'
She'd listened too long to the words in her head
That were placed there by somebody else,
A secret agenda misled her, I said:
'You need to believe in yourself.'

'I know they sound plausible, up on the hill,
They're experts at twisting your mind,
They plant their subversion so deep in your will
That you leave your own feelings behind.
But listen instead to the beat of your heart
And the things that you know to be true,
Don't let them divert you, confuse you or hurt you,
Hang on to the essence of you.'

'I need something deep to believe in,' she said,
'They offer that, up on the hill!'
'They offer submission to what they commission,
And part of their creed is to kill.
The secret of living is give and be given
Allow every man his own creed,
For nothing is certain, there's no iron curtain
Between what you want, or I need.'

'The rules are laid down in their Holy Book,
They tell me they come straight from God.'
'In whose estimation, or interpretation,
Which version, don't you think it's odd?'
The next time we met she was swallowed in black,
Her head bowed, three paces behind,
Her lips had been sealed, couldn't answer him back,
It was like the blind leading the blind.

Once All the Books are Gone!

They said that the Library was full,
Were going to pull it down,
They'd set up a whole new Google School
On the other side of town,
And nobody went there anymore,
It was bulging at the seams,
With every tome that had stood alone,
The source of a writer's dreams.

'What can we get from a paper book
That is not beyond a trace,
When just by tapping a couple of keys
We can pull it from cyberspace.'
They'd lost the sense of a cosy nook
On a languid day in June,
When curled up there with a thrilling book
They could drift and dream 'til noon.

The Library was a silent place
With its soot-stained yellow brick,
It rose a couple of storeys, and
The air in there was thick,
The shelves rose up to the ceilings, more
Than twenty feet in the air,
You had to call a librarian
To climb up a sliding stair.

But up above there were volumes bound
In a red and gold Morroc,
Their wisdom gleaned from the ages in
A perfect printed book,

Though some had never been taken down,
Their pages were pristine,
They waited patiently there for me,
A world that I'd never seen.

They closed the Library down one day
And nobody even cared,
The lights went out for the final time
The cost of the power conserved,
A gloom then settled between the shelves
That had held the stuff of life,
The books, still patiently waiting with
Their sagas of joy and strife.

I broke on into the Library
Through a badly padlocked door,
Made my way with the aid of a torch
On up to the second floor,
The tension there was electric, I
Could sense them asking 'Why?'
'Why has the world deserted us,'
And the books let out a sigh.

I looked on up and I saw a book
And it seemed to freeze my gaze,
Glowing softly it shimmered there
In a pale, blue misty haze,
I reached on up and I took it down
Though it tingled in my hands,
My mind lit up like a picture book
Of far and distant lands.

I laid it down and it opened up,
'The Book of the Universe,'

Then stars and planets poured out from what
I thought was an ancient hearse,
I heard some planetary music from
The deception that Neptune brings,
And floated up from the floor in there
Surrounded by Saturn's rings.

Knowledge flowed from the book to me
Though I couldn't catch it all,
It passed me by in a stream, just like
A glittering waterfall,
And then a voice in my head intoned
'You can pass this message on,
You'll never be able to smile again
Once all the books are gone!'

Dance with the Devil

She had met this handsome stranger
So she told me, at some dance,
And I knew then she'd be leaving me,
I didn't stand a chance,
She had not seemed so excited since
I'd given her a ring,
But I saw she wasn't wearing it,
It didn't mean a thing!

So I asked her where this dance had been,
She didn't seem to know,
She'd drifted in there like some dream
Where lovers always go,
I asked her who was there, she said
They'd glided round in grace,

And but for him, her eyes were dim,
She'd not recalled one face.

She hesitating, placed the ring
Back in my open hand,
'I don't have any choice,' she said,
'I knew you'd understand!'
I didn't, but I bit my tongue,
No point to cause a scene,
I hoped that she'd get over it,
But something was unclean.

I sat and moped at home awhile,
She'd cut me to the quick,
I'd planned my life around her,
Marriage, children, all of it,
But then I felt resentment rise
And choke me to the core,
I'd need to see him, Damn-his-eyes,
See what I'd lost her for.

So I began to roam the streets
And watch her, though unseen,
To hide in handy bushes, just
To find out where she'd been,
Then one dark night she ventured out
And walked, as in a trance,
I followed at a distance as
She went to join the dance.

The gates were flung wide open to
A long, curved gravel drive,
A house with gothic columns, where
The gargoyles looked alive,

I didn't see another soul
As Anne had ventured in,
But ballroom music filled the air
With subtle hints of sin.

I sidled to the ballroom and
I hid, as best I could,
While phantom figures whirled about,
Transparent through each hood,
The only solid forms I saw
Were first, my trancelike Anne,
And something evil on the floor
That could have been a man.

That could have been a man, I said
Despite his long black cloak,
The horns that grew from out his head
That looked just like a goat,
The tail that flicked behind it with
A barb of polished steel,
It could have been a man, I said,
But no, that sight was real!

Behind Anne was a marble slab
With bloodstains, from before,
A pale and polished altar that
Was raised up from the floor,
He took Anne in his arms, began
To sway and dance her round,
'You're dancing with the Devil, Anne,'
I screamed, and held my ground.

He roared, and turned his evil face
To glare where I was stood,

My heart stood still inside me, like
My heart was made of wood,
Then Anne began to shriek, her eyes
Now seeing what I saw,
Pulled back, and disentangled from
Each evil crablike claw.

I don't know how we got outside,
I only know we fled,
With terror stricken eyes and hearts
We thought that we were dead.
That house went up, a puff of smoke
Amid a demon roar,
Now Anne won't dance, no handsome stranger
Tempts her anymore!

Distance Never Lies!

The cottage in the country
Had become my main retreat,
From the chaos of the city,
From its never ending beat,
From the traffic and the steeples
Of the people and their cares,
I could leave it all behind me
When I went to ground out there.

It was just an hour's driving
Through some shady country lanes,
Round the far side of a mountain
And by cultivated plains,
Until sheltered in a valley
I could spy our cottage roof,

And my tension would release me
When arriving there, with Ruth.

There was little of the comfort
That we take for granted there,
Just a worn old wooden table
And for each, a shaky chair,
With an ancient cast iron heater
And a kettle on the hob,
We had the whole world beaten,
It was like a gift from God.

At dusk we'd wander hand in hand
Out past the Pepper trees,
When the heat of day was cooling
With a gentle valley breeze,
But lately I had sensed out there
That something must be wrong,
I couldn't quite get over it,
The feeling was so strong.

I waited 'til the morning, then
I paced the ground outside,
I hadn't been mistaken, though
My memory had lied,
I thought there'd been just sixteen paces,
So I told myself,
From cottage to the Pepper tree,
But now, there was but twelve.

I hesitated speaking out,
Then mentioned it to Ruth,
We've always been wide open
And there's nothing like the truth.

She came and paced it out with me,
I think she thought I lied,
Then went back in the cottage and
She sat right down, and cried.

We spent a pensive week out there
And noticed how the floor
Pushed up in different places where
It raised, and jammed the door,
And cracks were re-appearing where
I'd fixed them long ago,
The cottage walls were leaning
And I said, 'I told you so!'

We paced each day the garden from
The cottage to the trees,
The changes were so slight we prayed
And Ruth would mutter, 'Please!'
But one day when we paced it from
The Peppers to the den,
'It's not twelve paces anymore,'
I said, 'It's only ten!'

'So what's the explanation, John?'
Ruth said, before we left,
I didn't have the answers, I
Was feeling so bereft.
'There's something scientific
Going on, beyond our ken,
The world has started shrinking,
And it has to do with men,'

'Perhaps the outward motion of
Our growing Universe,

Has stopped at last, and now the thing
Is moving in reverse!'
I only know our one retreat
Has shrunk to half its size,
The trees are at our old front door,
And distance never lies!

The Witch of Aberdare

She stood in front of the mirror, staring
Combing her long dark hair,
A black cat jumped on her shoulder, purring
The Witch of Aberdare.
She took in the curve of her fulsome lips
And the dimple in each cheek,
'Why can't I find a lover for me?'
But the mirror didn't speak.

She'd watched the girls from the village, keeping
Trysts with the ones they loved,
As hand in hand they kissed on meeting
Down in the darkening wood.
But nobody sought out Alison Gross
Where she stood by the wishing well,
Dropping her pennies in hopes that any
Would lure a man to her spell.

Her mother, Isabel Ingpen once
Had been raped by Jonathon Dread,
But then had spelled by the wishing well,
Put him in a garden bed.
She'd witched him into a barren seed
But the evil in him came through,

Sprouted there as a deadly nightshade,
Tall, and blocking the view.

She told her Alison, on her honour
Her father had come and gone,
'But better avoid the Belladonna
You don't know where it's from.'
She taught her all of the witchcraft rules
Of philtres, potions and spells,
'But try to avoid the world of fools,
And men, who fancy themselves!'

But Alison had a disposition
For loving, though no-one saw,
The teacher who gave her impositions,
The boy who stood by the door,
The Baker's lad and the Butcher's boy
And the gardener, mowing the green,
But nothing would turn their heads her way
She was Alison Gross, unseen.

She sighed and cried as she cast her spells,
She wept as they sauntered by,
So deep in love with one another
And gazing up at the sky,
But Halloween was a day away
And Alison formed a plan,
'I'll weave my spells out in the heather,
I'm going to get me a man!'

The children were out, were trick and treating
As Alison took her broom,
She flew to the local witches meeting
At Heatherdale, under the Moon,

She looked at the other witches there,
So old, so sad and alone,
She swore before she was old as they
She wouldn't be left a crone.

She slipped away and she left the coven
Then stripped off her hat and cloak,
She lifted the cauldron off the oven
Went down to the giant oak,
The young were dancing and dunking apples
She wandered into the throng,
And a young man said with his laughing eyes,
'This is where you belong.'

He danced her under the Hunter's Moon,
And he stole the witch's heart,
She knew, without a potion or philtre
They'd never be far apart.
She holds a baby high on her hip
As she combs her curling hair,
And her lover stays, to trade her kisses
The Witch of Aberdare.

Born for Raising Hell!

He'd always been a schoolyard bully,
You want to know the truth,
He picked on those too young and silly
To stand up to the youth,
He'd ducked the boys in the village pond
And he hurt the girls as well,
And had a tattoo on his chest,
'Born for Raising Hell!'

He didn't learn, he was much too dumb,
He didn't see the need,
He couldn't tackle a simple sum
Or spell, or write or read,
But he thought the world had owed him some
So he took it, when he could,
And robbed his innocent victims by
Wearing the coward's hood.

The police would carry him into court
And the judge would let him go,
'He's had a difficult childhood, so
We must be fair, you know!'
And he would laugh when he got outside
And steal the nearest car,
He thought that he was invincible,
Some sort of rising star.

He'd hang with others as dumb as him
Who lived by a borrowed creed,
Adopt a type of a uniform
By growing an ugly beard,
They'd take the gifts of the welfare state
And would swear to tear it down,
'The time will come that we change the laws
When our army comes to town!'

He tamed a silly, submissive girl
And he beat her black and blue,
Then made her cover from head to foot
So her bruises didn't show,
He taught her to be subservient
To fulfil his every need,
And quoted God, with an iron rod
"Obey' shall be your creed!'

He went to fight in a foreign war
And at first they held their ground,
They slaughtered populations to
Strike fear, in every town,
But a barbarous army like their own
Appeared, and refused to yield,
And he was taken a prisoner
Out there, in a foreign field.

He thought he was going to lose his head
As he'd taken heads, before,
But they were a little more barbarous
In the way that they fought the war,
'We're sending you back to meet your friends,
But you won't have time to yell…'
Then strapped him onto a missile,
'There you go… Go Raising Hell!'

The Party Prank

There isn't a sign, there isn't a trace
Of Isabel Groom on the planet's face,
She stalked from the room in a great distress
With a foot long tear in her party dress.

'I shouldn't have come, I shouldn't have stayed,'
She said to the Under Parlourmaid,
'I should have remembered, Elizabeth Krank
Is fond, too fond of the Party Prank.'

'She came in a dress, with tassels in blue,
The same as the ones I was wearing, too,

I saw the glare that she gave me there
With the self-same comb in her party hair.'

Elizabeth went to the party cake
Staring, like someone barely awake,
She seized the knife from the cutting board,
Turned to Isabel Groom, and roared:

'How dare you wear that comb in your hair,
And a dress that no-one was meant to share!'
She flared, and slashed in that candle-lit room,
And tore the dress of Isabel Groom.

While Isabel spun, and grabbed at her wrist,
And bent it back in a sudden twist,
They say that she bent it more than she should,
And Elizabeth Krank was sputtering blood.

The knife was embedded, deep in her throat
And Elizabeth screamed, a long high note,
'I knew your party would be a mistake,
And now you've bled on the party cake!'

There isn't a sign, there isn't a trace
Of Isabel Groom on the planet's face,
She stalked from the room in a great distress
With a foot long tear in her party dress.

On the Other Side of the Door

She came back home from a morning class
And she thought to find him there,
She called for him in the morning room
And she climbed the wooden stair,
She called him up on her mobile phone
And she said, 'Where are you, Sam?'
His voice came nervously, in reply:
'I don't know where I am!'

The signal crackled, then faded out
And it came back in again,
She heard him mutter and try to shout,
His words reflected pain,
'I don't know how to get back,' he cried,
'That door down by the stair,
It opened up and it shut me out,
When I looked, it wasn't there!'

'There isn't a door by the stair,' she said,
'There isn't a door at all,
You must have fallen and hit your head,
There's blood on the stairway wall.'
'It's true that I must have cut myself
When the door had swung ajar,
But the house has gone, I've moved along,
And I don't know where you are.'

'Well tell me how I can find you, and
I'll get some help to search,
I might have to call an ambulance
If you've fallen off your perch.'

'This isn't a joke, I'm not insane,
But my world has turned about,
I tell you the door just disappeared
When it closed, and shut me out.'

'I'm out in the woods, beside a stream
With a girl that looks like you,
I know she's not, but she says she is,
And her name is Mary, too!
She swears that she's the original
And that you must be a clone,
She told me about the guy you meet
When you're safely on your own.'

Then Mary shook and she went quite pale
And she said, 'It isn't true!
There was a fellow that came my way
But I swear, he looked like you.
He had me fooled for a moment there
But I knew it when we kissed,
And then I thrust him away, and said
'Your lips don't taste like this!''

He breathed a sigh as she wiped her eye
And he heard her cry on the phone,
'I shouldn't have doubted you, my dear,
But I've been so long alone.
Our lives had drifted apart, so much
That I wondered if you cared,
We allowed ourselves to be led, instead of
The love that we should have shared.'

'Look for the door by the bottom stair,
When it opens, come to me,

Then we can be together again
As good as it used to be,
We'll live the life that we should have lived
Before, when our love was true!'
'Don't ever question my love,' she said,
My only love is you!'

A door came shimmering into view
At the bottom of the stair,
And swung out wide, on the other side
Was her twin, she would declare,
She pushed on through, and into the house
As Mary went through the door,
And turned to look, as the building shook
And sank to the forest floor.

Then Sam had taken her in his arms
As he had, when they were young,
And spun her dancing between the trees
As she laughed, her eyes had shone,
While up in the house, the clones had stared
For their love had been a sham,
'We're not going to make it now,' he said,
'I don't know where I am!'

The Parchment Scroll

From the time the land had fallen away
He could only see the sea,
And the billowing sails, the wooden rails
And the halyards, struggling free,
While a silence gathered beyond the creak
Of the masts, that seemed quite odd,
As up in the crows nest he could see
The massive domain of God.

For out to the far horizon, there
Was nothing to catch the eye,
But the heaving swell that he knew full well
And the vast expanse of the sky,
They merged in a distant thin blue line
On the curvature of the earth,
That disappeared as the evening fell
And the stars were given birth.

And there in the glow of the hanging lamp
He heard the bells of the watch,
As they hauled on the final moonraker
Above the sky sail, top,
The bow bit in to the salty swell
As the frigate picked up speed,
And dipped and sprayed on the carronade
In a race for a monarch's need.

For down below was a courier
Locked in by a cabin door,
Who carried a secret parchment scroll
God speed to a distant shore.

Dressed as a pale midshipman, but
In truth, and without a lie,
The courier was a fretful girl
And the crew would have wondered, 'Why?'

Why take a girl on a Naval ship
Who would bring bad luck to the crew?
Nobody was supposed to know,
But he in the crows nest knew.
He'd seen her shower in a secret place
He could see from the top of the mast,
But kept his lip, for he knew the ship
Would be wrecked if the crew had guessed.

She came on out for a breath of air
Just after he came off watch,
Deep in the dark of the after deck
With the gun deck all awash,
A giant wave swept her to the rail
So he seized, and held her tight,
As the water dripped from her frightened face
And her hair shook out in the night.

'Pray sir, don't let them discover me,
I am only here for the King,'
He smiled at her in the darkness, said
'You must grant me just one thing,
A tender kiss from your perfect lips
And I swear, I'll let you be.'
She said, 'You swear?' and she kissed him then,
But a grumble rose from the sea.

And thunder off in the distance rolled
As the girl then turned and fled,

Back to her locked in cabin then,
Back to her cabin bed.
But lightning flashed, and a thunderbolt
Crashed over the masts and stays,
While the lightning flash destroyed the mast
Where he'd spent so many days.

The crew were cutting the mast away
And cast it over the side,
While he hung on to a rail and stay
As the ship tossed in the tide,
A shadow rose from the deep that night
A demon known to the crew,
'There must be a woman here on board,'
They screamed, 'but nobody knew!'

The seaman went to her cabin door
Then knocked, and she let him in,
'Your secret's out, you'll have to leave
If you want to save your skin.
I'm going to let out the painter now,
And set you out in a boat,
I'll join you there if I can, I swear
For this ship won't stay afloat.'

And somewhere out in that great domain
That God has kept for his own,
There floats a tiny clinker boat
With a couple, all alone.
The frigate lies in the heaving deep
On the bed of a fretful sea,
One kiss had cost a King his throne
And the loss of a colony.

The Cast-Off

She saw her friend on the Monday,
At the fountain, by the square,
Her skin had seemed to be glowing,
With the sunlight on her hair.
She said, 'What's happened to you, my girl,
There's an incandescent glow
That emanates from your features,'
And her friend said, 'You should know!'

They met again on the Tuesday,
At a Café near the Strand,
Her friend sat next to a pale-faced guy
Who reached to hold her hand.
'So this is your little secret,
You're a deep one, aren't you, Eve?
You could at least introduce us then!'
She said, 'Oh, this is Steve!'

She missed her train on the Wednesday,
But she heard from near and far,
'Eve has got her another guy
And he writes, and plays guitar.
We wonder how long this one will last
For she's not been true before,
Eve likes a bit of variety,
She's sure to show him the door.'

They passed in the street on Thursday,
And stopped for a bit of chat,
'He says he's writing me summer skies,'
And Steve was this, and that.

'Everything seems to be brighter now
There's bluebirds up in the sky,
I feel that I'm tripping on a cloud,
I never felt so high.'

She noticed the breeze on Friday,
Was as soft as featherdown,
When Eve had texted her love for him
From the other side of town.
'Whatever he writes for me is done
In the twinking of an eye,
But I'm starting to feel so restless, for
At best, he's a boring guy.'

She happened to see, on Saturday,
Her friend at the local ball,
And looked for the poet Steve, but he
Didn't appear at all.
Though Eve was dancing with someone new
While thunder rolled in the west,
'I cast him off, but he's there for you
If you want him, be my guest!'

The lightning flashed on the Sunday,
And Eve was soaked to the skin,
She beat on the door of Janet's place,
'For God's sake, let me in!'
Her hair was hanging in rats tails and
She cried, 'I'm really scared.
Steve is writing a storm for me
For he said, he'd really cared.'

The storm had gone on the Monday,
The clouds were fluffy and white,

As Janet walked to the corner store
And Eve came into sight.
Eve said, 'What's happened to you, my girl,
There's an incandescent glow
That emanates from your features,'
And her friend said, 'You should know!'

All Hallows Eve

They'd painted a cross on the door outside
To keep the devil at bay,
While Ann took care of the soul cakes that
She'd baked in a shallow tray,
The Jack O' Lanterns sat in a row
On a shelf to await reprieve,
As darkness fell on the House of Hell
At the last All Hallows Eve.

They'd whisked the wandering spirits out
With a witches broom of straw,
And placed a basin of milk outside
So they wouldn't come through the door.
The dead could re-visit their homes that night
At that one grim time of the year,
So they set the table, an extra place
Should the shade of a ghost appear.

Across the road was a cemetery
To which John would haste away,
And light a candle on every grave
To keep the dead at bay,
He placed a dozen on 'Hammer Jack'
As the murderer was known,

Who'd hung in chains through a drought and rains
Til at last, his dust had flown.

But John had a muttered confession as
He lit up the candles there,
'I didn't mean you to hang, old man,
But I was beyond despair.
When somebody pointed the finger, I
Was only relieved to see,
That though I murdered my mother, still,
It wasn't pointing at me!'

He staggered back to the house and stood
To watch his woman, Ann,
He'd often thought to confess, but then
It's not that she'd understand.
He'd only done it for her, he thought,
His mother was grim and old,
And threatened that she would put him out,
And Ann, out there in the cold.

Jack, an itinerent labourer
From a cottage across the way,
Had liked his mother and visited her
When the deed was done that day,
There was blood on his fraying overalls
And blood on his front and back,
When he staggered out of the house, some say,
So they blamed him for the attack.

When John lit the Jack O' Lanterns he
Then placed them out in the yard,
Hoping that they would fend them off,
The ghouls from the devil's guard,

But just on the stroke of midnight
He grew pale at a distant howl,
From out in the moonlit cemetery,
Though Ann said, 'It's an owl!'

But then came the long and heavy tread
Of a pair of boots he knew,
Sounding on the verandah, while
The door had opened, too,
And standing there in the doorway
Was a dead man with a list,
A Jack O' Lantern sat on his head,
And a hammer in his fist.

Ann was crouched in a corner when
The police arrived, first light,
She babbled about some 'Hammer Jack',
Was right off her head with fright.
And blood was spattered on every wall
From John, who lay where he fell,
While 'Hammer Jack' was back in his grave,
Was done with the House of Hell!

Sister Switch

Annette, she was a Worthingham
And Karen, she was a Lee,
But both of them were adopted
In the war, in '43.
They pulled them out of a rubbled house
But their folks, they couldn't save,
And so they grew as the sisters two
With the common name, Palgrave.

As sisters, they were like chalk and cheese
Though the neighbours didn't know,
They said that one was the milkman's
And the other, Lord Mulrow's.
For Annette, she was a saucy tart,
Was the wilder of the two,
While Karen, she had a stately mien
With a haughty, grand purview.

They fought like cats through their teenage years
Would curse and swear, conspire,
Annette destroyed Karen's underwear
While Karen burned hers in the fire.
The mother was pale, and frail and ill
When she asked them both to go,
'I don't have to keep you anymore,
I adopted you both, you know!'

The news hit home like a thunderbolt,
They looked in each other's eyes,
'You mean, we're not really sisters, Hell!'
It came as a great surprise.

Karen went to her room to brood
Annette was flooded with tears,
'Why weren't we told, it seems so cold,
We should have known that for years.'

So Annette got a cold water flat
While Karen lived on the Square,
Then Annette got herself pregnant, but
Nobody seemed to care.
The boyfriend didn't appear one day
And she knew that he was gone,
She drifted into a deep despair
As time went travelling on.

She got so big that she couldn't cope
And she thought to take her life,
And then there came a knock at the door
Just as she raised the knife.
She groaned and whispered to go away
As she lay flat out on the cot,
'It's Karen here, it's your sister, dear,
I'm the only one you've got!'

She'd brought a parcel of food with her
And a daffodil layette,
'I couldn't choose between pink or blue,
Not knowing it's gender yet.'
They hugged each other and burst in tears
For a love they hadn't shown,
While caught in an unknown falsehood, but
Their sisterhood had grown.

Dark Portents

The end was nigh, he scanned the sky
For portents, dark and deep,
He'd sensed some troubled signs within
While tossing in his sleep.
He told his wife to pack some things,
The least that they would need,
But she said, 'You must leave alone,
I'm staying here, God speed!'

He found he couldn't change her mind,
No matter that he tried,
He told her of the darker times
That he had sensed, inside.
But she was quite content, she said,
'In fact I'm quite serene,
I shall not run before the tide,
It may be but a dream!'

The Castle walls with hallowed halls
Held shadows grim and bleak,
Where muttered shades from former days
Would flit from moat to keep,
From tower, to hall, to bedchamber,
He cast his nervous eyes,
Where even in the flagstoned floors
He thought, 'There evil lies!'

The evening skies were tinctured with
A weird orange glow,
And then the Moon rose up above,
A baneful, blood-red show,

While winds that howled like none before
Now clattered at the eaves,
And whispered down the chimney's core,
'God help the one that leaves!'

He wandered round the halls at night
And shook in some dread fear,
At sounds of chains, and distant pains
Deep in his inner ear.
He stood up at the battlements
And scanned the dark surround,
Where gargoyles leered, to spout their cheer
All on the hallowed ground.

'But surely you must hear them, Maud,
They're plain, so plain to me!'
'I only hear the chirping bird
That flits in yonder tree.
Perhaps your mind has been disturbed,
You need to rest at night,
I'll lock you in the Castle Keep
Until your dreams take flight.'

That night, asleep, but fitfully
He heard a horse's hooves,
That clattered in the courtyard, echoed
With its iron shoes.
And then he heard his wife, who whispered
Like some painted whore,
'He's almost driven mad, I've locked
Him in, and barred the door.'

Then like a charm that runs its course
And sets its victim free,

He knew that she'd been feeding him
With Belladonna tea.
He waited for an hour, and then
Burst hinges on the door,
And sought his wife's bedchamber
Where her lover felt secure.

'I told you I'd sensed darker times,
Such darker times, for you!'
He said as he approached the bed
And ran her lover through.
He raised the sword that dripped with blood
Then stood with drooping head,
While she went pale, to no avail,
In moments, she was dead!

The Isle of Gods

The passengers from the 'Bold Dundee'
Were sick as they crawled ashore,
Tossed about in an angry sea
By the God that they knew as Thor.
He'd beat his hammer along their hull,
He'd roared as the thunder clapped,
And ripped the sails from the forward stays
As the sheets and the masts collapsed.

The tide had hidden the rocks from view,
A mist had obscured the shore,
The captain thought he was sailing free
As he'd always done before.
But the ocean swell in its mystery
Hid atolls of murk and myth,

That never appeared on a sailor's chart
Where the Gods of old still lived.

The ship had shuddered and holed the bow,
Rode up, and sank at the stern,
The swell burst over the after deck
Drowning the crew in turn.
The passengers on the steerage deck
Were swept clean over the side,
Onto the rocks of a thousand wrecks,
But only a few survived.

By dawn that few had struggled ashore,
But the rest of them were dead,
Were floating out on the turn of tide
To rest on the deep seabed,
But Robert Young and his wife Jeanine
Were cast right up on the land,
And so was Emily Wintergreen
And the lad called Adam Shand.

They woke to an alien sunrise,
In a strange, pale purple mist,
And a sound came down from the mountainside
From a thousand years of myth.
A pale white horse bore a surly man
Who was ten feet tall to his head,
And roared, 'Now bow before Woden, or
By Odin, you will be dead!'

Then striding noisily through the trees
That grew right down to the shore,
Came a giant man, a hammer in hand
Who roared, 'You can call me Thor!

What brings you here to our hideaway,
To disturb our God's redoubt?
We left you, hundreds of years away,
Yet now, you seek us out.'

Each one of them bowed, and touched the sand,
'We don't know why we're here.
We didn't plan it,' said Adam Shand,
'It wasn't our idea.'
'You turned away from us,' Woden roared,
'Sought other gods to please,
Once you were praying to us for help,
Would beg of us, on your knees.'

'I swear we've never forgotten you,
You're with us, all of our days,
For Woden, you are our Wednesday now,
And that is eternal praise.
While Thor is our every Thursday,
Every week that he comes around,
And Tiw, well he's become Tuesday
So you're lost, but you are found.'

The Gods stood back, and then conferred,
'We're going to let you go,
But only because you honour us
With your calendar, if that's so.'
A longboat, free from the wreck came in
And the four of them climbed aboard,
Then waved goodbye to the Isle of Gods,
But at sea, they thanked the Lord!

The Old Man in the Park

The old man sat on the long park bench
Where the children used to play,
He seemed to be harmless, sitting there
Though he'd be there every day.
His pockets were always full of sweets
And he'd smile a kindly smile,
But mothers would huddle nervously,
They suspected him of guile.

'What do you think he's up to,' said
One mother to her friend,
'I've read some terrible things about
Young children and old men.'
'Can't you see that he's harmless,
He's so old, and frail and sick,
He's just like a kindly grandfather
Who walks with a walking stick.'

'He shouldn't be handing out those sweets,
We don't know what's inside,
What if it's something horrible
And one of the children died?'
'You need to become more trusting,
He's out here in the light of day,
I hope that he didn't hear you,
That's a terrible thing to say!'

He smiled and nodded, and fell asleep
Sat back on the wooden seat,
His overcoat had seen better days
And so, the shoes on his feet,

He woke when the children whooped about,
Swung high on the rusty swings,
Tempted the children with his sweets
And to some, he muttered things.

'What did the old man say to you?'
One whispered to her son,
"He asked if I wanted knowledge, if
I did, then he'd give me some.'
'You're not to speak to him anymore,'
The woman cried, in fear,
It isn't right that he fills your head,
By rights, he shouldn't be here.'

She went to sit on the wooden seat
And she grabbed him by the sleeve,
'What do you mean by 'knowledge' then,
I think you ought to leave!'
'I mean no harm, I'm a kindly man
And I love those children dear,
I'd give my all to be young again
And I feel young when they're near.'

She nodded, said that she felt ashamed,
And patted him on the arm,
Then got up, leaving her son to play
She'd lost all sense of alarm.
The boy was tempted again by sweets
And the old man grabbed his hand,
'Just stare right into my eyes, my boy,
I'll take you to fairyland.'

The old man's eyes were hypnotic when
He stared, and soon glowed red,

And then the little boy trembled as
A lifetime flowed in his head,
The old man smiled, and his hand relaxed
As the young boy turned to go,
'At last,' he capered, and danced about,
And the old man sank back, slow.

The mother came to collect her son,
He was nowhere on the green,
She went to the old man on the bench,
'Where's John? You must have seen!'
The old man struggled to sit upright
And held out a trembling hand,
'I've waited ever so long for you,
But I don't think I can stand!'

The Courtship of Sisters Three

There were sisters three, and they all were free
In a town called Tavistock,
Freer than they would want to be
As they stared at the Town Hall Clock.
'Our time is running ahead of us
They will soon call us 'Old Maid',
Said sister Jill to the younger Phil,
And the eldest one, called Jade.

'So why don't the menfolk look at us,
We're not that hard on the eye,
Certainly better than Betty Watts
Who married the stable guy.'
'I danced with him, did you know?' said Phil,
'By God, he's a clumsy oaf,

He kept on tripping over his boots,
And stamped on all of my toes.'

'I had a line on the fisherman,'
Said Jill, 'and I thought I'd win,
I'd give it a month or two to set,
And then I would reel him in.
But Nancy Croft got her hooks in him
And I see they've tied the knot,
I said, 'but you were going with me!'
He said, 'Oh! I'd forgot.'

Then Jade had turned with a waspish look
And she said, 'Well, look at me!
I'm the eldest and should be wed
By rights, the first of three.
There's only a single guy in town,
He's the only one that's left,
I heard him say he's going away,
He's an army boy, called Jeff.'

But Jill and Phil said, 'He's not yours,
It's the one that gets there first,'
They were in favour of drawing straws,
But Jade had stamped and cursed.
They said they'd ask him around to tea
They'd cook up muffins and toast,
And then they'd see what they all would see,
By whom he talked to most!

He came attired in his uniform
His scabard by his side,
Placed his sword on the mantelpiece
Where Jade stroked it with pride.

'My, but you're a fine gentleman
And I see you play the fife,
How sad, you'll march to a battle cry
Without a beautiful wife.'

He sat perturbed, and he looked at them,
At each one in their turn,
'If only there were three of me,'
He said, but his cheeks had burned.
The sisters jostled to catch his eye,
Were heated and dismayed,
'I know a way we can settle this!'
And Jill had reached for the blade.

She swung the sword and before they knew,
The soldier lay in halves,
She'd cleft him, clean through the waist, and then
She'd cut off both his arms.
To Jade the head and the torso went,
To Phil, arms worn like a shawl,
Which left Jill what was below the waist,
(She had the most fun of all!)

The Attic Rats

'There were noises up in the attic
When I arose today, Maureen,
Have you been storing your batik
Up on the shelves, for the shelves aren't clean!
I said you shouldn't go prying there,
There is nothing up there to see,
Just things I cast from a hazy past
Before your marriage to me.'

'I keep all my art and craft downstairs
In the cupboard, next to the door,
You've watched me folding my batik there
So what would you ask me for?'
'I only wondered,' her husband said,
'Those scrabbles, they could have been rats,
More reason never to venture there…'
'I'll bring in the neighbours cats!'

She smiled, and blew him a kiss just then,
They hadn't been married long,
They'd worked together for six long months
When she only knew him as John.
But after the office party, and
That cupboard, under the stairs,
A half a jug of Bacardi, and
They knew, the future was theirs.

She heard the scrabbling overhead
On a Sunday, lying in,
And what seemed like a rattle of chains
Though she thought, it couldn't have been.

John Dean was out at the supermart
So she scrambled out of bed,
Pulled down the ladder and mounted it
To the attic, overhead.

The hatch slid back from a faulty catch
And she peered, up into the gloom,
There were spiders webs and rusty beds,
And dust, in that grim old room,
She saw what looked like a cabin trunk,
Padlocked, and covered in chain,
And another trunk with an open lid…
She climbed down the ladder again.

At lunch, she mentioned the sounds she'd heard
And she watched her husband's face,
He seemed quite distant, then perturbed,
Got up and began to pace.
'You haven't been up in the loft, Maureen,
That attic is out of bounds!'
'Well listen to you, the stern John Dean!
How do you think that sounds?'

They didn't talk for another day
But her anger was aroused,
While he went up to the attic twice,
Mad at the scene he'd caused.
'I didn't mean it like that,' he said,
It's just that it's full of dirt.'
But she shrugged off his excuses, she
Was playing at being hurt.

She searched the house for the padlock key
That had locked the trunk in chain,

Then finally found it on his ring,
And slipped it off again.
She waited until the coast was clear
With John Dean not around,
Climbed the ladder and opened the trunk
With the key that she had found.

Just as she went to raise the lid
His head appeared in the hatch,
'Sorry it's come to this, our kid,
You're about to meet your match.'
The lid went up and she looked aghast
At the woman, speared with a knife,
'Maureen, please meet Deborah Dean,
She was my former wife.'

She pulled the knife from the woman's throat
And she pointed the blade at him,
'Don't think you'll ever do that to me,'
Her voice was dour and grim.
'That open trunk is your future home,'
He said as he locked the hatch,
'You'll jump right in and you'll close the lid
When you hear the giant rats!'

Strange Pathways

The gardens are laid in rows and lines
Laid out like a colourful maze,
The gates are open from eight 'til nine,
All week, and Saturdays.
But Sundays they open the gates 'til ten
They are lit by coloured lights,
I like to wander the strange pathways
But prefer to go by night.

I tell my Sally she ought to come
But she never has, 'til now,
Her head is always stuck in a book
She's what you might call highbrow.
One Sunday night, she said she'd come
We got to the gates by eight,
The lights were twinkling in the groves
And the Moon had risen late.

We walked by the beds of petunias,
Snapdragons and daffodils,
The heady perfume was rising up
And strange, but it gave me chills.
We took a fork where the wood was dense
With natives, bushes and trees,
But Sally tripped by a eucalypt,
And ended skinning her knees.

We sat on a garden bench nearby
And mentioned how quiet it was,
The pathway there was a yellow brick
Just like the Wizard of Oz.

We thought, 'We're the only ones in here,'
By ten, but she couldn't walk,
I said, 'We'll wait 'til the gardener comes,
We'll sit on the bench and talk.'

We sat for over an hour out there,
We sat discussing things,
Mother-of-pearl, the state of the world,
The cost of engagement rings.
But then a shadow had passed us by
Behind a hedge and a tree,
And out there popped the head of a man,
'Are you two looking for me?'

He couldn't have been but four foot two,
But hidden behind the trees,
His body never came into view
But he had two pointed ears.
I told him Sally had skinned her knees
And she couldn't walk just then,
He said he'd send for his volunteers
'But beware the Pathways Men!'

An hour went by and the lights went out
We began to fear the dark,
Then three young misses in party dress
Danced up from the outside park.
'We've come to carry your lady home,
Follow us if you may,'
Then plucked poor Sally out of my arms,
And danced down a strange pathway.

I don't know why it escaped my eye,
It hadn't been there before,

I tried to follow but found myself
Entangled, both foot and claw.
My path was blocked by three strange men
Linked up, to stand in my way,
'Don't think to enter the faery glen
Or your woman will waste away.'

I've searched the gardens, I've searched the grounds
I've searched in the nights and days,
I've called for Sally a hundred times
And lost myself in the maze.
But late at night there's an eerie sound
Like someone playing a lute,
Down at the end of some strange pathway
Where they grow forbidden fruit.

The Buried Past

The photos lay in a pile of dust
They'd gathered under the bed,
They'd not seen the light of day for years
Were neglected there, instead,
The wife found them with the first spring clean
And she dumped them in my lap,
'Who is the girl on the Honda Dream,
And the guy in the leather cap?'

I must have shot her a funny look
As we guys are wont to do,
'A girl I must have been going with
About twenty before you.'
She picked the photo out of the pile
And she brushed it on her skirt,

I thought, 'Oh, here we go again,'
Her face said she was hurt.

'How come I've never seen her before,'
She was getting close to tears,
I snatched the photo out of her hand,
'It must be fifty years!
I can't recall the time or the place
And I can't recall her name.'
She punched me once on the shoulder, said:
'You ought to be ashamed!'

That photo sat on the mantelpiece
And it stared at me for weeks,
A bonny girl with a pouting lip
And the wife gave me no peace.
It was, 'Just what did you talk about?
What did she used to say?'
I said, 'I can't for the life of me
Remember a single day.'

She served the hot-pot up stone cold
And the gravy didn't move,
I think she mixed it with concrete just
To show she didn't approve.
I said, 'I was only twenty then,
That snap was way back when,
We've been together for forty years,
Why drag her up again?'

'You've kept her a secret all these years,
That photo, under the bed,
How do I know you're not in touch?'
I said, 'She's probably dead!'

I racked my brains for a memory
But all I could see were thighs,
Pert young breasts and a petticoat
And a twinkle in her eyes.

But still I couldn't recall her name
Or a single word she'd said,
Only the scent of her sweet young breath
As we rolled in her parents bed,
She'd clung to me on the pillion seat
As her skirt flared out, and streamed,
Down at the back of Fletcher's Wood
On the back of the Honda Dream.

'I want to know what you did with her,
Though it doesn't matter now.'
(I'd fallen for one of those tricks before,
The wife's a devious cow!)
I thought of the day the fun had gone
When we lay, looked up at the sky,
'Ah, now I remember what she said,
One word, just one… Goodbye!'

The Headland Wreck

There was sadness in his towering form
As he walked the windswept beach,
The clouds were louring overhead
And the weed cast up was deep,
He had to walk where the tide came in
On a narrow strip of sand,
And darting surges caught at his feet
With their floating contraband.

The wreck of the ancient 'Neptune Glyph'
Embedded in drift was there,
Huddled under a looming cliff
With a trace of its last despair,
But rust had eaten its plates away
To the sound of the wheelhouse bell,
Where a Master and his daughter lay
'Til the ship became a shell.

But now he skirted the rusting ship
And he seemed to hear her voice,
The daughter, in her personal hell,
She'd been given little choice:
'Why did you take me out to sea
To avoid my mother's plan,
She'd said that we would be leaving you
For you're such a brutal man!'

Then a rumble grew in the rusting hulk
As the wind caught at the stern,
Rattling through the throat of a man
With a sound like someone burned,

'I had to keep your mother from you
For she's such an evil witch,
But she sewed a spell for a rising swell
And added the final stitch.'

The man on the beach could hear the roar
That rose from the rusted shell,
Of a storm that raged in the world before
And hurried them both to hell.
'Why did you have to take the life
Of the mother that might have been?'
He cried aloud at the rusting shroud,
'I'm left adrift in a dream!'

A voice replied in a rising scream
Then died away to a croak,
'I raised the storm, but I didn't mean
For my daughter dear to choke…'
The man turned back on the way he came
And left with a parting tear,
As a woman up on the headland watched
Him fade, and disappear!

Teaser

'I begged you not to go to the lake
For I knew that he'd be there,
Whenever we'd go to the lake before
He would come out, sit and stare,
He lived in a cabin, made of wood,
Was a woodsman, through and through,
But the hairs rose up on the back of my neck
Each time that he stared at you.'

'You wore that little bikini top
And the g-string pulled up tight,
I said that you'd catch your death out there,
It was cold, and nearly night,
But I saw you bridle at every glance
As he sat on his porch out there,
Then you swayed on down to the waters edge:
'To get a fresh breath of air.''

'If only you could have seen yourself,
You looked like a sad man's dream,
While he would twitch on his garden seat
Like a cat that had choked on cream.
I'd call you in, but you wouldn't come
Though I'd watch through the window pane,
And you would titter, and he would laugh
As you wiggled his way again.'

'What makes you fall for these burly men,
Could it be that they're so uncouth?
Their manners say they haven't a brain
So could it be faded youth?

You'll never be twenty-one again,
Nor even remember when,
And if they knew what you'd want to do
They'd hide in the fields and fen.'

'I begged you not to go to the lake
I can't trust you on your own,
The police have got your description now
We'll have to be moving home.
His jugular was punctured they said,
There wasn't a drop in his veins,
And yes, you're ten years younger again
But a hundred and ten remains!'

Following Jane

He'd stared at the silver screen so long
He thought he was going blind,
For a fortnight after his wife had gone
He thought he would lose his mind.
She'd snatched her purse from the window ledge
And said that she'd not be late,
'I'll just call in to the grocery store,
Then call on my sister, Kate!'

An hour went by and he scratched his head
While watching the cricket score,
Then two, and three put the sun to bed,
He went and stood by the door,
The Moon rose up at eleven or so,
It shone on an empty street,
And Kate replied to his mobile call,
'I've not seen Jane for a week!'

There wasn't a lot he could say to that
For Kate would have played it straight,
She wouldn't lie for her sister Jane,
She had enough on her plate.
A drunken husband, threatening her
Each time that he laid one on,
And Kate had whispered to Jane, 'I wish,
He'd pack up his things, be gone!'

Sam went to report to the police next day,
One lost, or wandered or strayed,
(The cop had smirked to his mate out back,
'Perhaps she went to get laid?')
'It's not like her, she's a homely type,
But something has gone amiss,
She left three bags at the grocery store
And she's not done that, 'til this.'

Once back at home on the Internet
He checked on her Facebook page,
Her smiling face looked back at him yet,
Making him more dismayed,
A man had posted a Timeline rant,
Had posted the previous day:
'I love you Jane, and I'm deep in pain,
I'm coming to take you away.'

The face of the man was indistinct
Was hidden in deepest gloom,
He must have taken the photograph
At night, in a dim-lit room,
The name that he used was 'Love-Will-Out'
But surely that couldn't be,

For Jane, he thought, was a simple soul,
'She wouldn't be false to me!'

He caught a glimpse of her now and then
As he wandered, page to page,
She'd left a trail as she trawled back when
And he felt a gathering rage.
A 'like' on a friend she used to have,
A comment that made no sense,
'I need a map' was the one remark
That had kept him in suspense.

'I don't know where,' she'd written up there,
Elsewhere, 'or where I am.'
'Somebody's following close behind
But I keep looking for Sam.'
Snatches of words that made no sense
He would see as they flashed on by,
And through the runnels of Facebook tunnels
He'd see that same grim guy.

So still he stares at the silver screen
Though he thinks he's going mad,
She seems to be there on the Facebook scene,
(In a way, that makes him glad).
But he'll never rest 'til she comes back home
To end that feeling of pain,
Whenever I ask if he's coming out,
He says, 'I'm following Jane!'

Trick or Treat

When I was a child, at Halloween
I'd go out to trick or treat,
With Pam, and Sam, and Wriggly Ann
Just us in the dark, cold street,
We'd knock on the doors of folk we knew
And they'd give us a sweet, or cake,
But those who wouldn't come to the door,
We thought they were cruel, or fake.

We'd look for a gnome, or garden tool,
We'd sneak right into their shed,
Stand up a rake, and play the fool
Stick a pumpkin there for its head,
And then we'd giggle and run away,
Go to the house next door,
And sometimes, eating the proffered cake
We'd laugh at the neighbour's roar.

We'd finished the street one night, and turned
To a place called Shady Lane,
It wasn't a place we'd often go
For the folk there were insane.
They hated children, they hated pets,
We thought that they'd ate our dog,
Had lured it off on a misty night
When the town was covered in smog.

'Let's trick or treat the Lavorsky's,' said
The pipsqueak, Wriggly Ann,
'Only if you will knock on the door
While we stand back,' said Sam.

The house was dark, there wasn't a light
And the Moon was hid in a cloud,
It loomed up there in the darkness like
A monster, wrapped in a shroud.

She knocked three times and we all stood back
Were getting ready to run,
With only Ann on the welcome mat
We thought he might have a gun.
The door had creaked and a hand shot out,
Grabbed Wriggly Ann by the scruff,
Then hauled her in and the door slammed shut
And Pamela screamed, took off.

I looked at Sam and he looked at me
As we both stood still, in shock,
'Maybe they're going to have her for tea
Like they did with our poodle, Jock!'
We skirted round on the garden path
Til we came to their rustic shed,
Opened the door, and there on the floor
Was Mrs. Lavorsky, dead!

Her eyes were wide, and shone in the dark
Her jaw sagged open and slack,
Her hands in a rigor mortis claw
Were raised, as if to attack.
And Sam had screamed like a little girl
(He never could live that down),
He fainted, fell right there on his back
On Mrs. Lavorsky's gown.

Her husband didn't know she was dead
Til the police came round that night,

But then he left her, there in the shed
For the hearse to collect, first light.
While Wriggly Ann was safe inside
Was stuffing her face with cake,
That Mr. Lavorsky'd laid on out,
The last that his wife would bake.

The Enchanted Manor

The Georgian Manor in Ripon Town
Had seen far better days,
The chimney pots had fallen down
And the windows, scarred and crazed,
The paint had peeled from the cedar door
And the ivy climbed untamed,
From the days of the aristocracy
The house was re-arranged.

There were flats and a communal kitchen
But no carpets on the floor,
The walls were damp and the paper peeled
In strips, from the old décor,
When Jennifer took an upstairs flat
She shuddered, 'It won't be long.'
But things in her life had taken a turn
With everything going wrong.

She lay on the iron poster bed
And she cried herself to sleep,
Ever since her engagement went
All she could do was weep,
The future, bleak and forbidding now
Held nothing but fear and tears,

It yawned ahead in her misery,
An aeon of wasted years.

At night, the gloom would descend, a pall
Would settle upon her room,
She'd lie awake to the mutterings
That seemed to come from the tomb,
The manor had once been bright and gay
With Lords and Earls, and Dames
Plucking at hammered dulcimers
While playing their wooing games.

And standing off in the corner was
A wardrobe, made of teak,
The doors were locked, there wasn't a key
It was just some old antique,
Or that was what she had thought at first
'Til her interest fired her mind,
And she levered open the doors one night
To see what there was to find.

She found there what was a treasure trove
Of gowns and hoods and capes,
Of silken skirts with their bustles,
Party masques for their escapades,
Muslin dresses and bodices
That Jennifer gaped to see,
That ladies wore all those years before,
And whalebone corsetry.

She felt a hidden excitement while
Surveying the gorgeous past,
And then an ineffable sadness that
Such grandeur didn't last,

The woman that wore these party gowns
Was laid in an ancient grave,
Along with her beaus and suitors all,
The clothes alone were saved.

One night she weakened, and tried them on,
They seemed like a perfect fit,
Over the laced up corsets when
She donned a satin slip,
She chose a gown with a turquoise hue
With a bustle of ribbon and lace,
While the gas lamp that had never worked
Lit up, to reflect her face.

Then music wafted under her door
From a dulcimer and lute,
A wistful song from an old spinette
And a Love song from a flute,
She thrilled to enter the passage where
The gas laps, in a row,
Played their light on the central stair
And the dancing, down below.

She floated to the head of the stair
As her gown trailed on behind,
And wondered as she descended what
Enchantment she would find,
The dancers stopped, and they looked at her
As she joined them on the floor,
And one said, 'Here is the Faery Queene,
We'd best make fast the door.'

A fine young man in a tailcoat came
And he bent to kiss her hand,

From white cravat to his doeskin boots
He was quickly in command,
He whirled her breathless, into the throng
As the dancers wheeled and spun,
Risen up for this one enchant
That her dressing had begun.

But after one in the morning she
Began to fear and doubt,
The tapers happened to flicker and
The gas lamps all went out,
The dancers started to fade away
To return to where they came,
'Til only she and the young man stood
In the glare of a single flame.

'They're happy now that you brought them back
Though the hours were swiftly spent,
They sleep again in their graves where they
Have aeons to repent.'
'But what of you, must you join them there,'
As she clung to him the more,
'Not I,' he said, 'for I'm not yet dead,
I live in the flat next door!'

The Paper Girl

Her picture was in 'The Courier',
A beauty with auburn hair,
I must admit I was taken in
As I sat alone, to stare.
Her eyes met mine with a knowing look
For her gaze was so intense,
Only a print in a newspaper,
I was making little sense.

I screwed the paper and tossed it out,
At least, it hit the bin,
But later I would scrabble about
For the piece that she was in.
I smoothed the paper and put the pic
Where it would be safe, and keep,
But found I still was thinking of her
At the sharp end of the week.

She showed again on the social page
Of that dreary rag, 'The Sun',
Was standing there in the background of
Some wedding that was on,
Again I scissored the picture out
And I put it with its mate,
But hadn't a clue just what to do
It began to feel like fate!

I asked around at 'The Courier',
I asked about at 'The Sun',
But nobody seemed to know where she
Could be, though she seemed like fun.

'She's always there in the background where
The photo's all get shot,
Then after the shoot is over, first
She's there, and then she's not.'

I started to hang about in clubs
And the places she might be,
I needed to salt her tail so I
At least, could set me free,
Her image was always staring, glaring
Stuck in my mind each day,
And then, I couldn't get off to sleep
So I'd curse the night away.

Her face popped out of a magazine,
A poster, there in the hall,
Standing behind some advertising
Blurb, on the old sea wall,
I went along to the Seaman's Rest
Thinking to have a drink,
And not too far, but along the bar
I saw… Well, who do you think?

I walked up behind her, shaking, quaking,
Tapped, and spun her around,
'You wouldn't believe what I've been through,
I've finally run you to ground!'
She smiled, and patted her auburn hair
'Well, would you believe, it's true!
Since I saw you staring into the page
I've been looking for you!'

House!

The windows up on the second floor
Peered out through the mist at dawn,
Through what seemed a couple of eyelids,
Peeping out, when the blinds were drawn,
They scanned to the far horizon
Past the billows and foaming waves,
As if to seek a solution
As they scowled from their architraves.

'How long, how long,' was the question that
Had hung in the air for years,
How long to a sure destruction like
A fabric, when it tears?
The sea surged up to its doorstep with
The king tide at its peak,
And whispered its evil mantra, 'House!
You haven't another week.'

The House had stood five hundred years,
It had seen them come and go,
The coaches bringing their ministers
Of church and state, below,
Armies had been sequestered there
Beneath the sheltered eaves
Conspiring to hide the redcoats 'til
The rebels made them leave.

It had sheltered friend and foe in there,
And had made no judgement call,
Its spacious rooms had been welcoming
To anyone there at all,

But now that its greatest enemy
Was surging at the lea,
'Who will come to my aid at last
To save me from the sea?'

The time was once when the sea lay back
A mile or so from the shore,
But long decades of its slow attack
Saw it conquer, more and more,
Its progress so very gradual
That some generations hence,
Each single lifetime lost just yards
From its seaward farmland fence.

A wall of sticks and boulders rose
That the sea had overcome,
Had buried under its surges while
The work was being done,
A hill of sand and flotsam that
Was bound by bush and tree,
But the sea reclaimed its contraband
Washed the sand back out to sea.

And now, five hundred years had gone
The tide lapped at the brick,
And softened the old foundations as
The window-eyes looked bleak,
The king tide then had abated and
Sank back, to mutter its lack,
'Have no fear,' it grated, 'House!
For I shall be coming back!'

But with the sea lying dormant,
Men approached with great machines,

With bulldozers and graders and
Huge tip-trucks in a stream,
And when the sea had resumed again
With its king tide of assault,
It beat forlorn on a concrete wall
With pathways of asphalt.

The windows up on the second floor
Peered out through the mist at dawn,
Through what seemed a couple of eyelids,
Peeping out, when the blinds were drawn,
The rain had hidden a couple of tears
As the House had heard men say:
'We have to preserve our history,
And keep the sea in the bay!'

The Secret Wood

There are places still on this planet where
No man has ever trod,
That lie so deep in the undergrowth,
Put there by the grace of God,
And denizens lie there, watchfully
In guarding their holy place,
Intruders enter but never return
As part of the human race.

The earth entangles and trips their feet
When they stray from near and far,
And vines entwine in a blink of time
To tether them where they are,
While briars inject as they're taking root
Seep poison into their veins,

To leave them dank with their eyes so blank
With what human thought remains.

I saw you wandering aimlessly
Too close to the place of God,
And followed you inconspicuously
Or you might have thought it odd,
And when you stumbled and almost fell
At the edge of their secret wood,
I found and slashed at the vines that bound
In that alien neighbourhood.

I lured you out of the convent walls
And I sought to take you home,
You raised your head in confusion, said
That all roads lead to Rome,
I said, 'You're throwing your life away
For the drear of a lonely cell,
But life is there to be lived, my love,
Or all roads lead to Hell.'

The Penguins came to collect you, tried
To bind you with former vows,
And flapped their wings at your reason
Using what force the law allows,
I slammed the door in my silent war
On their medieval taint,
And hoped you'd say that you'd marry me,
Though I never wanted a saint!

It's been a year and I see you stare
Each time that we pass their gate,
Wondering if you should be there
But I thank God, it's too late,

Our daughter bubbles with life, and grins
As a child of God, she should,
I'd rather her path was paved with sins
Than lead to their secret wood.

Beside the River Wye

At Tintern Abbey I set my bait
To fish in the River Wye,
I'd only been an hour, I swear
When the girl came floating by,
Her dress spread out, a fine brocade
And some lace about her hair,
I almost drowned when I reeled her in
And fell in the river there.

I pulled her up on the river bank
And she lay, and softly sighed,
I felt a strange relief, and thanked
The Lord, I thought she'd died.
But her eyelids gave a flutter then
And she looked at me apace,
'Would you be one of the Abbot's men?
There's no mark upon your face.'

'I only came to fish,' I said,
'And I like what I have caught.'
The look she gave me made me blush
For it set my jest at naught.
'The Abbot Gilbert lies within
By his candle, book and prayer,
The pestilence has found his sin
For he knows, he's dying there.'

I thought her speech was quaint and old
Like an echo, lost in time,
I thought, 'I've never seen one so fair,
If only she was mine!'
But she sat, and moved away from me
And she said, 'You mustn't touch,
For death has stained this fine country,
It may have you in its clutch.'

'But I only came to fish,' I said,
And, 'there's nothing wrong with me;
Yet you float down the River Wye
And will end up in the sea.'
'I chose the cleansing waters so
To avoid the pestilence,
The dead lie in the fields about
And it spares no eminence.'

'My husband, Guy Fitzherbert bleeds
In the Abbey's ante-room,
His pilgrimage denied his needs
And the Lord will take him soon.'
I stared at Tintern Abbey's shell
Standing gaunt against the sky,
'You must be catching a fever,
We must go and get you dry.'

'I needs must be on my way again,
Good sir, I wish you well,
But leave this place if you'd rather live
Than enter the gates of Hell.'
My mind caught at some thing she said
And a thought, then so sublime,
I asked the girl, 'What year is this...?'
'Thirteen forty-nine!'

Family Secret

He knew that there must be something wrong
From the time he brought her home,
His mother had turned her back when he
Announced her as Alice Frome,
'She lives in the vale by Abbeville
Where I met her at the dance,
Mother, you have to greet her for
This may be a true romance.'

His mother had pursed her lips, and turned
Surveying her up and down,
'You shouldn't get carried away,' she said,
'There's plenty of girls in town.'
Then Alice blushed, was taken aback
By this woman's cruel jibe,
'What have I done to you,' she said,
And the lad, he almost cried.

She left, and swore she'd never come back
And the lad had left as well,
His mother watched throught the curtains
Knowing she'd put her son through hell,
'Just what in the world were you thinking of?'
He said, when he came back home,
'I meant, she wasn't the one for you,
That girl, that Alice Frome.'

'You don't even know her,' said the lad,
'You wouldn't know what she's like,
She's good at art and she's awful smart,
She's not some terrible dyke.'

'I know her sort, I've seen them before
And she's not the one for you,
Take your mother's advice, my son
Or she'll tear your heart in two.'

But he went to meet her secretly
On the odd nights of the week,
And when his mother had asked him where,
She found that he wouldn't speak.
He woke one Saturday morning late
His ankle chained to the bed,
'You won't be going to visit that girl
Unless I'm already dead!'

He cried and ranted and called for her
But his mother wouldn't come,
She locked the door to his bedroom
And the windows, every one,
She brought his meals but she wouldn't budge,
'You will lie here 'til she's gone,
'Til she has another boyfriend, and
I'll bet, that won't be long.'

She kept him chained for a week in there
Then Alice came round to call,
She beat and beat on the panelled door
Then sat on the old stone wall.
'I'll not be leaving 'til you come out,'
She yelled, so the neighbours heard,
And soon, the mother had let her in,
Face grim, but her eyes were scared.

They sat and talked in the kitchen there
For an hour, or maybe more,

Then Alice walked with a tear-stained face
Slamming the old front door,
His mother let him off from his chain
But she made him sit downstairs,
'That Alice Frome said leave her alone.'
He said, 'I know she cares!'

'It isn't a question of caring, son,
But a question of what is right,
You just can't marry that Alice Frome
And I'll tell you why tonight.
I felt let down when your father left
And I had an affair or two,
And then I fell, you should know as well
For I am her mother too!'

'I had her swiftly adopted out,
Burying past mistakes,
I couldn't care like I cared for you
We do whatever it takes.
But I knew the people that took her in
And I've watched her from afar,
You couldn't marry your sister, son,
You'll find there's a legal bar.'

'Why didn't you tell me this before,'
He cried as he turned his back,
'I didn't want to reveal my scar…'
He said, 'It's too late for that!
We think she may be expecting now,
It's not just affecting you!'
'She'll have to have an abortion, son,
That's what she's gone off to do.'

He left the house in a flood of tears,
His mother cried in the dark,
The worst had come of her secret fears
She was losing her son, her Mark.
A week went by then they found the two
Curled up in a four-post bed,
Their pale young faces were tear-streaked,
A brother and sister, dead.

Deny, Deny!

He met her under the willow trees
That grew by the valley creek,
He hadn't been able to visit her
For the best part of a week,
She patted her horse's neck, and sighed,
And waited for him to say,
The one thing that she feared the most,
That he might be going away.

But in his eyes there was only love
As he reached, and kissed her hand,
'We mustn't be seen down here by him,
I need you to understand,
He rides abroad since he found us out,
And says he's looking for me,
His stablemaster has said, no doubt,
I'll hang from the nearest tree.'

'He wouldn't dare,' said Jennifer Moss,
'My father would have him lashed,
He's always been too quick with his fists
He killed a man in the past.'

'But never paid the ultimate price,
He thinks he's above the law,
I'm keeping my flintlock pistol primed,
My powder dry by the door.'

'He hasn't said anything yet to me,
So how do you think he knows?'
'Your stablemaster has seen us kiss
By the barn where the river flows.
Beware, my love, he's a dangerous man,
Will settle his score with me,
But then, with you, he will seek revenge
Denial may set you free.'

'You must deny that you care for me,
Deny that our lips have met,
Deny, deny is the only course
That may make the fool forget.'
'My heart is bursting with love for you,
I couldn't deny what's true,'
'You must, my love, or the scene is set,
I fear what he'll do to you.'

He rode away to his hilltop farm
And he locked and barred each door,
While she rode off to the Manor House
Where her husband paced the floor.
'I fear my wife is a Jezebel,
So the stablemaster tells.'
'I have no interest in men,' she said,
I'm married to one from Hell!'

He turned on her in a rage at that,
He believed his master spy,

While she continued to hear the words
Of her love, 'Deny, Deny!'
'I'll spare his life if you tell the truth,
If you don't, the man is dead,'
She weakened then and admitted it,
She once had been in his bed.

He sent his louts to the Hilltop farm
And they dragged him out in dread,
They tied him to the back of his horse
To the Manor House, they led.
The husband leered when he saw him there,
'Well, your love has you redeemed!
I'll let you live in your bleak despair…'
His love was hung from a beam!

The Basement Stair

I'd rented out the basement of
A house I used to own,
I hated renting places
I preferred to live alone,
I wasn't good at choosing all
The tenants I would get,
And this guy was a doozy
The most eccentric of them yet.

But I must admit, the money
Paid the mortgage, right on time,
And I looked toward the future
When the house, it would be mine,
So I put up with his foibles
And his funny little ways,

He would sit down in his basement
And would disappear for days.

He had a little doctors bag
He wouldn't be without,
With signs both astrological
And Druid runes, no doubt,
He always took it with him
When he wandered down the street,
Come skulking back, and talk about
The weirdo's that he'd meet.

I knew something was going on,
I heard both screams and moans,
Seep up from out the basement
With the creak of drying bones,
At night they used to wake me up
And I'd lie there in dread,
And wonder what that movement was
Beneath my poster bed.

One night I crept on down and stood
Outside the basement door,
And heard strange voices muttering
Not one, but three or four,
I heard him raise his voice and say
In tones both harsh and grim,
'I didn't say you'd have your way,
But you can enter him!'

A peal of ghoulish laughter then
Rang out behind that door,
I bounded up those steps, ran like
I'd never run before,

Then lowered down the steel trapdoor
That sealed off that stair,
And laid the carpet over it,
You'd not know it was there.

I put up with a week of thumps
And cries of 'let me out!'
But put my face close to the floor
And whispered, 'Hey, don't shout!
You keep those demons that you raised
Locked in your doctor's bag,
Or maybe they will enter you,
And then, if so, that's sad!'

I waited for those sounds to die
For upwards of a year,
Then poured a ton of concrete in
To seal that basement stair,
The house has sold, a Mr. Bould
Paid not enough, no doubt,
But said, 'there's not a basement there,
I'll have to dig one out!'

Five Hundred and One

The office was in a building that
You wouldn't have looked at twice,
In truth, it stood in a part of town
That wasn't very nice,
The blinds forever were drawn down tight
And were thick with stains and dust,
I wouldn't have sought a job in there
But I felt that I really must.

I was over a year on welfare, and
I knew that it had to end,
I'd lost all my self-respect, my car,
And I hadn't a single friend,
When this came up in a tiny ad
On the supermarket board:
'Be one of the Movers and Shakers,
Then put the Takers to the sword.'

My curiosity peaked, and I
Marched into the office grim,
An insipid girl was behind the desk,
'You'll have to talk to him!'
A man in an inner office sat
In a cloak and black cravat,
'We're needing another numbers man,
Do you think you're up to that?'

I said I was up to anything
For I didn't really see,
That there would be ramifications
And they would apply to me,

He showed me into an office with
A desk and a swivel chair,
Then pulling a ledger off the shelf
He set it before me, there.

'Your job is to add up the columns
Putting a total to each name,
Remember, you're only the numbers man
So you're really not to blame.
Then when you get to five hundred, tear
The page from out of the book,
A man will be round to collect it,
Let's just say, he's Dr. Hook.'

I didn't meet this mysterious man
'Til I tallied up more than three,
A Johnson, Sands, and an Adamson,
And a man called Jacoby,
They'd totalled just five hundred each
When I tore their pages out,
And Dr. Hook slid them into a book,
I said, 'What's it all about?'

'Never you mind, my lad,' he said,
'It's better you didn't know,
There are things that shouldn't bother your head
Until it's your time to go.'
But those names remained in my mind until
On watching the nightly news,
An Adamson died in a mighty wreck
And a Sands, from a faulty fuse.

I thought it might be a coincidence
And I put my mind at rest,

When the girl from work came visiting,
And she seemed to be distressed,
I'd thought that she was insipid, but
There was fire in her belly too,
'You know that the guy whose place you took
Is dead… So I'm warning you!'

She said that I had a page as well
In a book, kept under her desk,
'If you saw your column, adding up,
I think you'd get little rest.
For every page you give Dr. Hook
I add ten each to your name,
With that score of ten, you'll be just like Ben,
He lasted a year in the game!'

'He'd started fudging the figures when
His number was creeping up,
I'd warned him, like I am warning you,
But it wasn't ever enough,
An audit pushed him over the top
By adding a hundred points,
And the ten he'd skimmed then died with him
In that fire at the Pizza joint.'

My column is stuck, four-eighty-nine
At this moment, as I write,
I still believe I can fend it off
If I'm careful, keep it tight,
I sweat, while adding the figures up
Of a certain Dr. Hook,
His column tops five hundred and one
As I tear his page from the book.

Man in the Future Past

Long after a heated argument
With his wife in the afternoon,
Roger James had taken his angst
To nurse in the small, spare room.
She said he'd always lived in the past
But little he knew of today,
And what he knew had no further use
For the past had drifted away.

He said that the base of knowledge was
The things they learned from the past,
That all they knew in the modern day
Was built from the past, at last.
'There's not a single decision we make
That hasn't been made before,
And a study of consequence, you'll find
May stop us from going to war.'

'You crazy man,' was his wife's response,
'Your life is a pitiful lie,
What do you know of the price of milk
Or the cost of a shirt, tie-dye?
Does it matter that stamps were tuppence once
Or that petrol was three and six,
And what can enhance our lives today
From the knowledge you have of the Blitz?'

'You trivialise the argument,
Your feet are stuck to the floor,
You're lost to the thrill that knowledge brings,
You'll never be able to soar!'

So he took his gloom to the attic room
And he lay on an old camp bed,
His mind was filled with a sense of doom
As images raced through his head.

He knew he'd never been practical,
He kept everything inside,
She'd thought he was a wonderful catch
When first he'd made her his bride.
But the gloss had gone as the world went on
He was gradually left behind,
Sat in a nook with a cosy book
While she burnt the chicken, and cried.

He lay and sent up a silent plea
To the stars and the universe,
'If this is life in the present day,
Could the future be much worse?'
A crack appeared in the further wall
And a bell had tolled outside,
And when he walked back down to the hall
There was no sign of his bride.

Her things still lay where they'd lain before
But of her, there wasn't a trace,
The house was still, in the world outside
No sign of the human race.
He walked awhile on the empty streets
Where the cars were parked, and still,
But nothing moved, not even a dog
As he walked up, over the hill.

The buildings seemed to be all intact
With a single change, he swore,

The date had changed on the city bank,
One after the day before,
Just a single day in the future, he
Was leading the human race,
They hadn't arrived where he was at,
It was merely one day of grace.

He spends his time in the library
And walking the empty streets,
He knows they'll never catch up with him
'Til his wandering day's complete.
But now he misses his wife and kin
And everything of that ilk,
So spends an hour of his future day
On the prices of gas and milk!

Lady Jane

In the time of knights and chivalry
In the Castle of Grim Intent,
There lived the Baron de Romilly
That the King or the Devil had sent,
His knights were the scourge of the countryside
For they only dealt in pain,
Taxing the helpless peasantry
In the name of Lady Jane.

But Lady Jane was a prisoner
In a dungeon, deep and dark,
Gone were the days she'd ridden to hounds
In the castle's spacious park,
The Baron had taken the castle,
On a dark and moonless night,

He held a warrant from England's King
But that didn't make it right.

He'd slain Milady's pikemen,
Who had been the drawbridge guard,
Thrown their bodies into the moat
Left others, dead in the yard,
While Lady Jane on the battlements
Said, 'What brings the Baron here?
Your evil knights are the country's blight
So I would that you'd disappear!'

The Baron laughed in his ugly way
But his face was grim and sour,
He seized her, said he would make her pay
Then thrust her into the tower,
'You'll pay for this, I'm of noble blood,'
She had screamed, and cursed his name,
But he dragged her down to the dungeon,
And he tethered her there in chain.

His knights had raged through the countryside
Put yeomen and serfs in thrall,
They ran a sword through the village priest
And the Squire in the Manor Hall,
The countryside was awash with blood
As the Baron's rule held sway,
While Lady Jane had muttered in pain
'He will live to rue this day!'

She'd retained a wandering minstrel,
Who had played to pay her court,
And he was spared by the Baron's men
For the music that they sought,

But one night after a revelry
When the knights lay drunk on the floor,
He slipped away down an old stairway
With the keys to the dungeon's door.

He heard a weeping, as if in pain
And wandered along to check,
And found the prison of Lady Jane,
Released the chain from her neck,
They crept on out to the castle yard
And mounted two horses there,
Then galloped out through the drawbridge, leaving
The gaping guards to stare.

She roused the surrounding country,
'You have everything now to gain,
Pick up your scythes, and your swords and knives
And we'll show the Baron pain!'
They marched as a farmers army,
With bitterness at its core,
And slew the guards at the castle gate
And the knights that lay on the floor.

The Baron was dragged to the battlements
Where they'd fixed a sturdy rope.
He begged for Milady's indulgence,
But she gave him little hope,
'You're going to meet your maker,
For you've played the Devil's pawn,'
Then launched him into eternity
To the cries of the peasants scorn.

His corpse hung 'til it rotted away
While Milady held a feast,

In thanks to the local peasantry
That he'd cared about the least,
While her minstrel wooed with a tuneful song
Though his eyes cried out in pain,
From the dreadful love that he'd held so long
For his mistress, Lady Jane.

I Can Read Your Mind!

I think she came from a Gypsy Clan
Where Dracula spilt his blood,
All that way in a caravan
To live in a field of mud,
But she danced like a whirling dervish,
At the campfire by the sea,
While I looked on like a love-lost one
Each time that she looked at me.

She wore a bright red rose in the hair
That was long, and thick, and black,
And dangling golden earrings,
With a shawl across her back,
But I stood transfixed as she twirled and kicked,
I felt like a man who begs,
Her skirt flared out as she danced about
And all I could see was legs.

All I could see was legs, I said,
The legs of a country girl,
The fine and moulded calves and thighs
That had danced half round the world.

She smiled with a hint of mystery
As she flashed her cute behind,
And said, 'I know all your history,
For I can read your mind!'

She danced away in a sort of play
Now she'd got me on the hop,
I didn't know where to put my eyes
On her breasts, or eyes, or what!
She certainly was a buxom girl
But her legs had made me blind,
She kicked up high and she showed a thigh,
That said, 'I can read your mind!'

I hadn't much of a mind just then
It was all consumed with lust,
Why can a thigh make a grown man cry?
I thought it was so unjust.
A man could dance til the cows came home
But it wouldn't raise an eye,
While the other kind could make men blind
At the glance of a naked thigh.

I shook my head and I turned away
I couldn't take more of this,
If that, her wheeze, was merely a tease,
She'd cornered the world of bliss.
But she stopped her prance and her wild dance
As I walked off into the trees,
She followed me from the clearing there,
Kicking up autumn leaves.

I turned, as she was behind me then
And pressed her against a tree,

I said, 'Just tell me your Gypsy name,'
She said it was Chavali.
'Well, Chavali you're a teaser,
Are you really one of a kind?'
She raised her eyes to the northern skies
And said, 'I can read your mind!'

We wandered into the furthest woods
And we found a bed of leaves,
I couldn't tell you what happened there,
Though Chavali skinned her knees.
But now, today, it's a world away
And I'm not a man who begs,
For every time, she can read my mind
And flashes her Gypsy legs.

Talk is Cheap!

He'd worshipped her since Primary School
And through to the later grades,
He'd carried her books at High School,
And envied her escapades,
She was in demand with her Uni friends
And went with more than a few,
But always said, to make amends,
'I think I'll end up with you!'

So he waited for an eternity
For that all-committing kiss,
She plagued his dreams with what would seem
A life that would fill with bliss,

But she seemed to like her fun too much
And returned his engagement ring,
'I don't think I'm ready for that, as such,
It's only a freedom thing!'

But he stayed content, he thought she'd relent
When her fun-filled friends all wed,
Until the day she blew him away
And dropped him, right on his head.
She married a wealthy businessman
Had taken a giant leap,
He said, 'But you were promised to me,'
And she said, 'Talk is cheap!'

But he bit his tongue, she was still so young,
And he nursed his sad regret,
Her husband, he was a ladies man
So things might work out yet.
He went to all of their parties, and
He ran all her errands too,
So when, of course, it came to divorce,
She said, 'I'll end up with you!'

But she won a great big settlement,
And wanted to have some fun,
'I've done that housewife thing to the hilt,
Don't stress, don't force me to run!'
'You know I'd wait for eternity,
I'd walk to the stars for you,
I'd give my life to make you my wife.'
'Well, do what you have to do!'

He hung about on the fringes while
She played with a whole new set,

She flirted, went on her binges, and
He found he was waiting yet.
He cried all over the invite that
Had seemed to come out of the blue,
'We'd welcome you at the nuptials,
Of Elspeth and Gordon Drew.'

Gordon drove a fabulous Porsche
Worth over a hundred grand,
And John could only wave as they passed him,
Off to their fairyland.
But he followed along the old coast road
Though they left him in their wake,
At a hundred and twenty miles an hour
A second is all it takes.

He found them, hanging over the edge
Of the cliff at Dead Man's Tor,
A sudden move would help it to tip,
Crash down to the rocky shore.
'Please help, you said you'd walk to the stars
For me, this cliff is steep.'
'Too bad,' he said, while walking away,
'You should know that talk is cheap!'

The Will of God

'To whomever it may concern,' he wrote,
Hunched over an evening star,
'This, my last will and testament
For you, whoever you are,
I leave your planet, the universe
To face an unthinking fate,
I tried to guide, but your priests all lied
And repentance came too late.'

'I was the Lord of Creation, set
Each atom of you in place,
Designed and sculptured your godlike form
Placed heaven in every face,
I gave you animals, birds and bees
And fish in the waters deep,
Flowers and colours and stately trees
And that blessèd rest, called sleep.'

'I took the rib of an Adam, as
He slept in my garden home,
And made for him a companion, that
He'd never have need to roam,
But now you treat as a chattel, she
Who loves, do you think it odd?
That man is born of a woman, while
A woman was born of God!'

'I hoped and wished you would be content
With the home that I made for you,
I charged you just a peppercorn rent
That you would acknowledge my due,

But you turned from me and created gods
Of mammon, and things unclean,
You fought each other and played the odds
For you said I was unseen.'

'I couldn't reveal myself to you
While giving you all free will,
I hoped you'd do what you had to do,
Driven by good, not ill,
But how many false religions now
Have taken my name in vain,
Have turned me into an evil god
As my tears fall down, like rain.'

'You've stolen my nuclear secrets, though
You wouldn't know where they're from,
And rather than make some godly thing,
You've manufactured a bomb.
So I leave you now to your schemes and fate
For you failed to reck my rod.'
Now heaven is closed, the sign on the gate…
'Farewell, Best wishes, God!'

That Was Then…

I walked along a cobbled street
That echoed, clattered, at my feet
And thought of many feet before
Who'd walked this way, but nevermore.

Those cobbles always seemed like home
Had been there since the days of Rome,

My father led me first that way
And his as well, before my day.

Then back, as far as we can see
Those cobbles lay through history,
Though worn and scuffed to mark their age
As walkers shuffled off each page.

Each came, eyes bright, a will to win
A glow without, a fire within,
Determined each to make their mark,
Their headstones now loom in some park.

Their needs and deeds, it must be said
Are soon forgotten, now they're dead,
Though once it seemed their world was won
It shone and shimmered, then was gone.

And love loomed large in every tale
That walked those cobbles, made men pale
And listless, for the love they lost,
While candles lit each Pentecost.

And I think of those years gone by
That wrought from me a whispered sigh
Of love, I thought, that was well spent,
Was there at Christmas, gone at Lent.

And so I walk these cobblestones
That trip my years, and make old bones,
I turned, and lost that dream somehow,
For that was then, and this is now…

Heaven, Hell, or the Highway

Solomon thought he was doing well
His assets just grew and grew,
He had no moral imperative
While ripping off me and you,
He'd made a fortune in stocks and shares
And a little insider trading,
Had married, divorced, with a bit to spare
For his extra-marital mating.

He wasn't exactly a murderer
Though he'd peddled horse and hash,
If someone died he would say they lied,
He needed the extra cash.
He was at his prime and was feeling fine
At the age of forty-two,
When an evil bloke with a scythe and cloak
Said, 'I've been looking for you!'

The sudden shock was a heart attack
The pain caught him by surprise,
He thought he might buy him off, but saw
The implacable, staring eyes.
The guy said, 'I'm just the messenger,
You're going away, it's sad!
You'll have to leave it behind, you know
But you can't complain, you're bad!'

He found himself on an open road
That was either up, or down,
He thought, with the wisdom of Solomon
He'd try the high end of town,

But a clerk with wings at a Pearly Gate
Said, 'First you must come by me,'
Pulled out a plate that was headed 'Fate!'
'I have to check your CV!'

He read, and mumbled and held him there,
And whispered under his breath,
'This can't be right, you shouldn't be here,
You suffered an early death!
You haven't had time to mend your ways
But the rules are more than clear,
You've not enough points on the 'Goody' side
So you won't be welcome here!'

He pointed to way, way down on the road
Where there shimmered a reddish glow,
'They might be more than amenable
To letting you in, you know.'
So Solomon turned, his heart in his throat
And he made the long trek down,
To a surly goat in a pigskin coat
Who greeted him with a frown.

He tried to enter but, 'Not so fast!'
The goat had stood in his way,
'I have to check your CV you know,
Before you get in today.'
He read and mumbled and held him there
And whispered under his breath,
'There's not enough evil here to spare
With you guys from a premature death.'

'It's sad,' he said, 'but you can't come in,'
He said in a voice so gruff,

'You're bad, I see, but your history?
You're simply not bad enough!
I have to be able to justify
That you've earned more than you can handle,
It's a serious thing, for eternity,
To make you a Roman Candle.'

So Solomon found himself out in the cold
On a long and deserted highway,
With all of the others rejected there
Who'd said they would do things 'My way!'
If only they'd thought before they died
What they'd need for a clear admission,
The goat would have welcomed them all inside
As a lawyer, or politician!

Isle of the Dead

He'd lain off the island just a week,
It was really only a reef,
That thrust up out of the waters
Ninety miles from Tenerife.
It didn't show up on a local map
And he thought he'd heard it said,
'Be sure, if you think of sailing west
That you miss the Isle of the Dead.'

On the higher part was a grove of trees
He explored when he went ashore,
And hidden deep in the foliage was
A house, not seen before.
It was made of wood, and covered in vines
That acted as camouflage,

It couldn't be seen 'til you came up close,
And stood with the door ajar.

He thought it must be deserted, though
A garden was weeded out,
And then, as he had approached the door
He was pulled up short, by a shout.
'Who's this, who enters my private grounds,
Who's this, who plays with my head?
We never have visitors here, you know,
For this is the Isle of the Dead!'

He turned, was facing a sprightly girl
With a mass of auburn hair,
She wore a costume of paw paw leaves
That had made him stand and stare,
Her eyes reflected the brightest blue
Of the ocean, out in the bay,
And her mouth affected the slightest pout
As he wondered what to say.

A woman came through the cottage door
And she said, 'Come in, Narreen,
We never talk to the strangers, for
You don't know where they've been.'
Her manner was quite unfriendly as
She gestured to the shore,
'You'd better be making way, my friend,'
Then shut the makeshift door.

He slept on his vessel every night
But he came ashore at dawn,
Hoping to get the briefest sight
Of the girl, for his heart was torn.

He hesitated to call it love
But it grew, each time he saw,
Her figure appear from the grove of trees,
Or saunter along the shore.

She finally came to talk to him
And squatted to hear him tell,
Tales of the wondrous world out there
Of jewels and gold as well,
Her eyes grew brighter with every tale
And he said, 'You should come with me,
We'll sail on the balmy Autumn swell
And you'll see the world for free.'

Her sister came to the beach one day
And she took the girl back home,
'I think that it's time you sailed away,
We haven't the need to roam.'
But he came ashore the following day
And he lured the girl to his boat,
She seemed surprised at the size of it
And the fact that it could float.

He tried to sooth, as he raised the sail
'We'll just go out for a spin,'
But she was suddenly nervous, and
She asked that they go back in.
He thought that he'd made the girl his own
As they sailed from the bay, at last,
But then he noticed the withered crone
Who clung, in death, to the mast!

The Terror

He never came out in the daytime, though
He'd always come out at night,
I'd hear his feet, pass in the street
By the gaslamp's feeble light,
He'd peer through the frosted window glass
And I swear that he always hissed,
Whenever I opened the trap, he'd gone
A-swirl in the yellow mist.

We huddled under the chimney piece,
We huddled under the stair,
Whenever his steps were echoing
From here to the you-know-where,
I tried to protect my Carolyn
Who would shut her eyes and ears,
He had the power, for over an hour
To bring Carolyn to tears.

He'd come when the frost brought icicles
He'd come when the wind would blow,
He'd come when I left her tricycle
Outside, and covered in snow,
And then when the ice on the window ledge
Began to go crack-crack-crack,
She often hid, right under the lid
Where the firewood lay in a stack.

And then when the door blew open, from
A gust in the wind out there,
We'd lie, with fears unspoken
As the creaking rose up the stair,

Then Carolyn shrieked, while I couldn't speak
For hearing her cries and moans,
As terror spread, from under the bed
And chattered through teeth and bones.

I swore that he wore a big black hat
With a brim that covered his eyes,
Carolyn wrote that he wore a cloak
As part of his dread disguise,
But nobody would believe us, 'til
We heard he was coming back,
His hobnailed boots on the cobblestones
Approached, a-click and a-clack.

They'd slow, and stop by the outer door
Our hearts in our mouths, alas,
And then his shadow would fall right there
He'd peer through the frosted glass,
The knocker had an echoing sound
As he knocked, went rat-tat-tat,
And mother leapt to the door in a bound,
'Dear God! It's Uncle Jack!'

The Ruined Church

Whenever I ride in the countryside
On the further side of the hill,
I can see the new church steeple, rising
Over the fields and rills,
Then I venture down to the valley, on
The Little Newhampton side,
And see the wreck of the ancient church
And remember the day it died.

Its blackened stone lies wide to the sky,
Its rafters lie in the nave,
If God was passing that fateful day
He thought it too late to save,
The lightning bolt that shattered his cross
Went on to set it on fire,
The lectern, pews, of Reverend Buse
Conspired to burn on his pyre.

They found his skull, all covered in ash
But the rest of him had gone,
Had flown his soul with its blackened wings
To a feast on the Eve of John,
He was known to hold a Satanic Mass
On the night of the Witches Moon,
But the Bishop's men were hard on his track
And would have defrocked him soon.

His congregation was always sparse,
For the good folk stayed away,
They'd heard strange rumours of what went on
With the Squire, and the Widow Hay,

They locked themselves behind cedar doors
And called on the god of wrath,
With lighted candles, inverted cross,
Laid out on the altar cloth.

The evening of the lightning strike
The leadlight flickered and flashed,
And screams rang out in the early hours,
As a black cat hurried past,
For then the windows had glowed bright red
To herald a presence there,
While a deep, loud gutteral voice rang out
To foul and corrupt the air.

'Where are my churls and underlings,
My troglodytes and my trolls?
Tonight is the night of sundering
Each evil heart from its soul!'
The Squire burst out, made a run for it
And tried to leap on his horse,
But the old black mare took him back in there,
And somebody slammed the doors.

And that was when the lightning struck,
It flashed, and shattered the cross,
The blazing roof came tumbling down
And the Widow Hay was lost.
They never found the Squire or his horse,
But I think that's just as well,
They're probably roasting chestnuts, down
In the seventh circle of Hell!

Midnight

The hands are at eleven o'clock
There's an hour of life to spend,
I haven't looked since seven o'clock,
Where did it go, my friend?
We all were out there, having a ball
Or doing what had to be done,
And sleeping, mating, loving and hating,
Thinking that life was fun.

We had no thought of how far we'd come,
We laughed in the sun and rain,
And cried sometimes, we were overcome
With the thought of another's pain,
We left some friends on a different track
And our loved ones disappeared,
Lost forever, they won't be back
And the thought brings us to tears.

So what will we do with the days to come
That have dwindled down to a few,
Will we all forget, and despite regret
Keep doing the things we do?
There is just one thing we should mull upon
As we're drawn to the sky above,
That the maker gives and the maker takes
But the greatest of gifts is love.

So now I look in my lover's eyes
You've been faithful, good and true,
I wouldn't have got to eleven o'clock
If I hadn't been loving you.

You baked the bread with your loving hands
And I broke the bread for us,
But once that terrible midnight chimes
I'll leave on a different bus.

So let's be thankful for what we've got,
And everything that we've had,
The toys, the joys, the girls and the boys
And everything good and bad.
There's a greater plan in the universe
And it waits, beyond despair,
It's not the end in that tasselled hearse,
I'll be waiting for you, there!

The Gamekeeper

I'd brought my woman to live with me
In a cottage by Elmsley Wood,
We lived on pure and simple fare
For my wages weren't that good,
I bagged a hare and a stoat or two
With my ancient .22,
She skinned and cooked, and cleaned and looked
For something better to do.

'I'm used to the shops and supermart,
The bars, fast cars and fun,
I didn't know we'd be isolated,
Let's go back there, hun!'
I hadn't a job for two full years
And she knew that to be true,
'I only remember the city tears
When I couldn't look after you!'

We'd always been such a loving pair
When we lived outside the yoke,
With plenty of time for making love
In a ratty flat, and broke.
But once I became a gamekeeper
I had a feeling of pride,
'A man has need of his self-respect,'
I said, so Kathy sighed.

I'd do my rounds at the dawning while
The sun was lying low,
While she would sleep every morning
Spring or Summer, heat or snow.
Then I'd go out in the evenings when
The Moon was riding high,
Hoping to catch the poachers on
My patch, and being sly.

So Kathy began to go for walks
Each sunny afternoon,
She wouldn't stick round for lunch, or talks
And the cottage was filled with gloom.
I'd take my break in the afternoon
Either read, or take a nap,
And hear the crackle of twigs and leaves
As she came walking back.

I warned her not to go walking through
The depths of Elmsley Wood,
'There's a couple of shady characters
In there, up to no good.'
She said she'd taken it all on board
Just walked the nearer trees,

Listening to the songs of birds
And the hum of busy bees.

One afternoon she had gone, and I
Was not too tired that day,
So wandered deep in the wood where I
Might meet the rogue, John Gray.
I saw him out in a clearing, and
He had her in his clutch,
I thought that I must be dreaming for
She wasn't wearing much.

I turned, and hurried back home without
Them knowing I was there,
I had my heart in my throat, but was
Determined not to care.
The rage was building within me
For the woman who was mine,
I thought, 'How could she deceive me?'
But that evening was sublime.

She said that the larder was empty
Could I go and bag a hare,
I said, 'Just give me an hour or so,
I'll bag some thing out there.'
I came in late, and upon the plate
I tossed her John Gray's head,
'I couldn't find you a hare, I swear,
Just pickle that instead!'

Goblin Castle

'Why do they call it Goblin Castle?'
I asked my friend, Carstairs,
We sat, gazed up at the battlements,
'It's a hell of a way up there!'
I knew that the Lord and Lady Crane
Had been living there, forever,
'It used the be called the Castle Bleak,
But Goblin Castle... Never!'

He bit his lip and dismounted, and
We tethered the horses fast,
Went to sit by a hollow tree
And squatted, sat on the grass.
Carstairs had worked for the Cranes for years
So he knew the ins and outs,
Of every tittle and tattle there
In that massive, noble house.

'It happened just when the Lady Crane
Was only a maid in there,
Before the Lord had taken a shine,
And offered his hand to her.
Her name was Jenny de Quincey
From some distant, noble blood,
But all she had was the noble name,
Her folks were as poor as mud.'

'There were places there that she shouldn't be,
There were places that were barred,
The servants said that its history
Was more than battle-scarred.

They whispered rumours of little folk
Who had roamed about in the past,
Had stolen goblets and golden plate
But they'd all died out, at last.'

'She ventured down to the dungeons, where
They'd kept the local churls,
Back in the days of taxes, that
Were paid to the Lords and Earls.
She expected to find them empty, but
Then further along the hall,
She found a dwarf, just two foot four
Who'd long been chained to the wall.'

'The dwarf had a sickly pallor that
Looked green in that eerie light,
A monstrous forehead and bulging eyes,
And he gave the maid a fright.
He said he'd been chained a hundred years,
That he came from a local tribe,
'Of Goblins, Hobs, and Gnomes,' he sobbed,
But the rest had not survived.'

'Jenny was wearing a golden chain
That he came to the bars to see,
For goblins love the glitter of gold,
Are rabid for jewellery.
He snatched the chain and he backed away,
Clutched it against the wall,
'You'll have to bring the key to the cage,'
He said, and she was appalled.'

'She brought the key the following day
And opened the rusted gate,

She didn't know quite how strong he was
But she found out, all too late!
It wasn't only the glitter of gold
That the goblin had in mind,
But to draw a veil on part of the tale,
I think would be more than kind.'

'She luckily married the Lord that week
So it wasn't a total mess,
She started to show, that womanly glow
And the Lord had thought him blessed.
But the truth came out when the heir was born
With a face that glowed pale green,
With bulging forehead and flapping ears,
And the biggest eyes I've seen.'

'They keep him down in the dungeon, in
A cage, right next to his Pa,
While she's locked up in the tower room,
Has never got out, so far.
It used to be called the Castle Bleak
And it lived right up to its name,
But now it's called the Goblin Castle
Of Lord and Lady Crane.'

Stroke!

I'm sitting mute in my wheelchair,
They think that I'm deaf and dumb,
Since ever the stroke that took me out
Emboldened everyone,
The jokes that they told behind my back
They say straight out to my face,
They think I'll die of a heart attack,
I think they're a sad disgrace!

It's always about the money,
It's always about the gilt,
They think they're getting a fortune,
They're all hocked up to the hilt,
They think that my Corporation
Will soon be theirs for the take,
They'll shunt me out to the sidelines,
I think that's a big mistake!

If they think that I'm weak and dying,
They really don't know the man,
I built up a corporation
With the strength of these two hands,
I was out in the streets at fourteen,
I was selling and hustling then,
While they were sucking their mother's paps
I was out with working men.

Not one of them's done a hard days work,
They sit there, pushing a pen,
They've never raised blisters on their fists
That bled, oh, time and again,

They sit in their pristine offices
With a wall of framed degrees,
But never spent time in a filthy trench
With water, up to their knees.

When I'm left alone in the evenings,
I stagger up out of this chair,
And force myself to walk to the wall
And back, as I fight despair,
But I'm gradually getting stronger,
And my head's as good as it was,
I'll show these ignorant jokers
What it takes to be a boss!

I think they're getting impatient,
They want me out of the way,
I've heard them mutter between them,
That they'll speed my going away,
The one that I used to trust the most
Has sat in my chairman's chair,
He smirks and shirks all the daily work
While I can but sit and stare.

They're treating me like an imbecile
They're treating me like I'm mad,
They've draped a blanket over my lap
And don't realise, I'm glad.
They come at night with a plastic bag
And they place it over my head,
But out from the rug my Magnum looms
And then, Bang Bang, they're dead!

Our Parting Ways

'We must have entered the Latter Days
For the Moon has broken in two,'
Said Paul Maresh in the month of May
Of Twenty Twenty-two,
'I said they shouldn't be mining it
And drilling through to its core,
For now the Russians claim half of it
And the States have gone to war.'

'That nuclear bomb on Ohio left
A crater, big as a lake,
And I heard that Lake Ontario
Has flooded New York State,
The world is shifting allegiances
So we don't know where we are,
Since the Internet has crashed and burned
With my friends, both near and far.'

He went to the old style UHF
That he kept in his father's shed,
Checked that the aerials were up
And the generator fed,
For the power had gone for the second time
And they said, it won't be back,
With the power station the target in
That first, but brief attack.

He switched on channel 11 then,
Hoping to hear her voice,
Through shifting, drifting frequencies
He sat there, calling Joyce,

But all he got was a wailing call
To prayer, from a Dervish man,
Sent out to all of the faithful from
Some place in Pakistan.

He checked through all of the channels that
They'd used, back there in the past,
But mostly got a cracklng sound
From the swirling, nuclear ash,
His sister Joyce, having flown on out
To the States in the month before,
He thought was missing in Florida,
In the first week of the war.

Then a voice came through on channel three
That was lost, and fraught with pain,
'Is that the Paul Maresh I met
In June, on the Sydney train?'
His mind went back to the smiling girl
With the drawn out Texas drawl,
Who'd chatted, stolen his heart away
With her laughed, 'Be seein' Y'all!'

They'd kept in touch on the Internet
And she said she was coming back,
Preparing to give their love a fling
On some great Australian track.
But then the world had shuddered with
That first American bomb,
So now, as frequencies swirled, he said,
'Where are you calling from?'

He thought that she said from 'Boston', though
A crackle had interfered,

Maybe the word was 'Austin' back
In Texas, that he'd heard,
But then her voice was carried away
In a trans-pacific hum,
And the last few words he heard, she said
'I really love you, hun!'

Part of the Moon has crashed to earth
In the Gulf of Mexico,
With Texas drowned in a sea of mud
And the earth's rotation slowed,
But Paul Maresh in the Aussie Bush
Is clamped to the UHF,
Looking for Joyce and Linda if
It takes him his final breath.

Don't Come Here Anymore!

You caught at my understanding,
You shocked me right to the core,
I've not had a harder landing, than:
'Don't come here anymore!'
I thought that you must be joking,
But couldn't detect a smile,
My heart had missed when you said that this
Was coming on for a while.

I shook my head in confusion,
How could I have missed the signs?
You working, close in collusion
With your mentor, Matthew Grimes.
He promised you'd have a starring role
In a film he was going to make,

I said right then to be wary, when
He was probably just a fake.

He'd said he was a Producer,
I treated all that with scorn,
The only score that he'd had before
Was something to do with porn.
You shrugged, and said that you trusted him,
That he was your first big break,
And then, 'So what,' for he said you'd got,
Everything that it takes.

'Everything that it takes,' he said,
We know what he meant by that,
He wanted you topless, on the screen
With a cane and a tall top hat.
I didn't think you would go for it
But I see, how wrong could I be?
You've let the seed of ambition rule,
Confused it with artistry.

I toss and turn in my fretful sleep
And sweat in my bed at night,
For every dream is of you, it seems
And it puts my sleep to flight.
I can't tell whether it's real or dream
When I knock at your old front door,
And you keep repeating the same old theme,
'Don't come here anymore!'

The Crone Who Lived in the Well

'Where are the spirits of those who went
Before, do they still survive?'
I said to Alice who pitched our tent
Outside, in the cottage drive.
We couldn't sleep in the cottage then
There was still a mess to repair,
And rubble lay in the dining room
With dust, most everywhere.

We thought that we were so lucky then
For the cottage and grounds were free,
An ancient Aunt, called Emily Sahnt
Had left in her will, to me.
I'd never met her, the dear old thing
But I raised a glass to her now,
Despite the fact that her neighbours thought
That she was a right old cow!

They said that she was a witch of sorts,
Had given the evil eye,
Had grumbled all round the neighborhood
Had killed some pigs in a sty.
And out in back was a wishing well
Uncovered, that somebody found,
And that's where Emily met her end,
She fell in the well, and drowned.

I said, 'I'll clear it away some day,
The rubble that hid the well,
You never know what it might conceal
A tunnel that leads to Hell!'

And Alice shuddered as Alice does
Whenever I freak her out,
I love to tease her as well as please,
She knows what it's all about.

There wasn't time for the well just then,
The cottage was coming first,
We cleared a couple of rooms inside
Moved in, and Alice had cursed,
The paint peeled off from the ceiling and
It dropped in chips to the bed,
We woke, with bits in our mouths and ears
And Alice felt strange in the head.

She felt quite ill for a day or two
Was sick, confused for a spell,
I left her sleeping it off and went
To work in clearing the well,
I dropped a bucket into its depths
For the water, clear and chilled,
And used it up in the cottage then,
And kept the bucket filled.

The groaning started that very night
And a grumbling in the eaves,
I said to Alice, 'Is that you, Pet?'
Then I heard the crunch of leaves.
There were footsteps round about the place
And I lay, tensed up with fright,
I wasn't game to be venturing out
In the middle of that dark night.

Alice said she was hearing things
And I tried to calm her down,

We'd burned our boats in moving there
And couldn't go back to town,
She seemed to be sleeping a lot by day
And plagued with fears at night,
I wanted to do the best for her
What I did, it wasn't right.

We were using the water from the well
To wash, to cook, for tea,
I suffered from blinding headaches then,
I found, and so did she.
The pigment in her nails had changed
She convulsed, not once, but twice,
I said I'd bring in the doctor just
To get some sound advice.

Alice died in the morning, she
Lay still on the side of the bed,
I shook her a couple of times, she was
So cold, I knew she was dead,
The doctor sent for forensics, and
They checked the place, the well,
There was arsenic in the water there
And the ceiling paint that fell.

I'm lying here in the hospital
But I'm chained, and under guard,
The police think they have a murder case
And they say I might be charged.
But I had a dream of a rustic crone
Who was clutching Alice hard,
Who said, 'I don't want to be alone,
You can walk with me in the yard!'

The Final Rest

I was driving along the coastal route,
Looking for somewhere to stay,
A Bed and Board that was cheap would suit
In a nice secluded Bay,
But the weather broke on the seaward side
As the clouds came tumbling in,
So I had to pull to the side of the road
Next to a painted Inn.

The swinging sign said, 'The Final Rest'
And it creaked as the seawind blew,
With a skull emblazed on the painted crest,
Though rain impeded the view,
And what was left of an ancient wreck
Lay caught on the rocky shore,
Only a matter of yards beyond
The road, and the old Inn door.

I waited until the rain had stopped
Then made my way to the bar,
An ugly crone stood there alone
On her face, a terrible scar,
She leered and said, 'Would you like a bed,
For the storm's set in for the night,'
My mouth was dry as I wondered why,
That scar was a terrible sight.

I said that I'd stay for just one night,
Then stood, and couldn't but stare,
She said, 'I know what you're looking at,'
Reached up, and patted her hair,

She ran her finger along the scar
With a wizened, frightful hand,
'There were some once said I was beautiful,
Oh, the wondrous works of man!'

I dropped my eyes and apologised,
While taking the proffered key,
'I hadn't meant to be rude,' I cried,
'It's nothing to do with me!'
'That's what they always say,' she said
While leading me up to my room,
Way up there on the topmost floor,
It was dark, and like a tomb.

The room held a large four poster bed
With a canopy up above,
I shut the door and I sighed, 'There but
For the grace of the Lord above…'
The wind was rattling round the eaves
It was well set in for the night,
And I lay and mused on the woman's fate,
What a truly, dreadful sight.

I must have fallen asleep just then
For my soul was so depressed,
I didn't want to be stranded there
But at least I'd get some rest,
Then two o'clock in the morning I
Awoke, as my heart had raced,
The canopy had been winding down
Was pressing down on my face.

I wriggled out from beneath its hold
And struggled to get my breath,

I now knew what was 'The Final Rest'
It was nothing less than death,
I watched the canopy creep on down
Til it gripped where I had been,
It was nothing less than revenge on men
In a plan that was obscene!

Then nothing happened for half an hour
While I shuddered beside the bed,
I knew, if I had been lying there
The odds are, I'd be dead,
But then the bed had begun to move
To tilt on its side, real slow,
And then the floor, it had opened up
To reveal a tank below.

And there the bodies of seven men
Lay in a watery grave,
Suffocated in blissful sleep
By a woman that was depraved,
The man that inflicted that dreadful scar
Had taken her life and soul,
Had turned her into a twisted crone
The Devil had in his hold.

She finally entered the deadly room
And her eyes were dull, and blank,
I jumped on out and I seized her then
And threw her into the tank,
She didn't struggle, she didn't cry
She knew it would come to this,
But sank and stared from the water tank
As the floor closed, with a hiss.

Whenever I travel around these days
I always sleep in the car,
It's not so comfortable, that I grant
But it's safer now, by far,
I hear that 'The Final Rest' has gone,
Developers bought the site,
And built a massive hotel just there,
They call it, 'The Restful Night'.

A Christmas Tale

We moved on into this neighborhood
When we couldn't afford the rent,
So my pessimistic Uncle Jim said,
'Next step down's a tent!'
The house is set in the meanest streets
And the locals here are rough,
They'd steal the pleats from your mother's skirts
If they weren't nailed down, that's tough!

So we put a chain on the old front door
We put a lock on the back,
We nailed all the lower windows down
In case of a night attack,
We put 'hedgehogs' in the garden beds
So intruders would step on the nails,
And stay away from the window ledge
Like Peeping Tom in the tales.

'It's best we're prepared,' said Uncle Jim,
'The locals are all on drugs,
They break into houses on a whim,
Thinking we're all just mugs.'

He kept a cricket bat by the door
And a baseball bat in reserve,
'If anyone comes in here at night,
By God, we'll give 'em a serve!'

I'd stand my watch on the upper floor
If anything moved in the street,
And write it down for my Uncle Jim
On a crumpled, beer stained sheet.
I'd note the time by my digital watch
That had cost five bucks in the Strand,
'It's better for you, my lad,' said he,
You can't tell the time with hands.'

We crept on out in the dark one night,
He said it was Christmas Eve,
And took a saw and a flashlight out
Looking for Christmas trees,
We stole a tree from a neighbour's yard
He'd planted the year before,
'He'll never know,' said my Uncle, low,
He'll never get through our door.'

We dragged it back to our house, and left
An obvious trail of green,
I pointed it out to Uncle Jim,
'What if that trail is seen?'
He shrugged, and put on his thinking cap,
'I'll say someone stole our tree,
They dragged it along our garden path,
It's nothing to do with me!'

We stuck the tree in a bucket inside
Then dangled some paper chains,

And some ancient pieces of glitter, that
Were worse for the winter rains,
He found a little fat fairy, who
Looked like she was six months gone,
And stuck her up on the top of the tree
With a Goblin called 'Bon Bon'.

Lying in bed that very night
Something moved on the roof,
One of the rats from the neighborhood
No doubt, on forty proof,
I went and I woke my Uncle Jim
And we clattered on down the stairs,
Just as a pair of big, black boots
Came 'Crash' on the hearth out there.

I rushed and I grabbed the cricket bat
My Uncle Jim had a shoe,
This geezer dressed in a funny hat
Popped down, and out of the flue,
His suit of red was covered in soot
And he started to dust it off,
When I whacked him one on his big black boot
And he yelled, 'Hey! That's enough.'

But Uncle Jim had pummelled his waist
And belted him with the shoe,
I whacked him once on his fat behind,
What else was a boy to do?
Then Uncle Jim had grabbed at his beard
All wispy white, like floss,
Swung him twice all around the room
Then said, 'It didn't come off!'

We let him go, then we stood and stared
While he cursed and swore at last,
Then clambered back up the chimney piece
My Uncle said, 'What a blast!
I don't know what he was hoping to steal,
There's nothing in this old house.'
But looking out in the yard, I said,
'The garden is full of cows!'

They were funny cows with great big horns
Like I'd seen in countless books,
Tethered fast to a loaded sledge
Piled up with frozen chooks.
'I think we've made a mistake,' he said,
My poor old Uncle Jim,
And true, I've not seen the man in red
Since we almost did him in!

The Magnetic Girl

Who would have thought the storm would come
So soon, from a pale blue sky,
When the weather man said, 'Fine til noon,
And the afternoon, quite dry.'
But moisture fell in a feathery squall
On the morning of that day,
Blown from the top of an anvil cloud
Some twenty miles away.

By two o'clock, the cumulonimbus
Cloud had drifted in,
Its anvil top like a dreadful shroud
As black as the darkest sin,

And lightning crackled within that cloud
Before it was given birth,
And loosed in chains with the driving rains
As it found its way to earth.

We pulled the blanket off the beach
And we closed the hamper top,
As the wind picked the umbrella up
And bowled it, til it dropped,
While Helen stood with her hands on hips,
Stared balefully at the sky,
'Thanks, you ruined our picnic,
With never a warning, why?'

As if in answer to Helen's taunt
The lightning struck her tongue,
Her face lit up in a brilliant glow
As bright as the morning sun,
She stood for a moment, paralysed
Then she toppled onto her face,
I'd never seen anyone crash to earth
Face down, with such little grace.

I rolled her over the sand, face up
And I gave her mouth to mouth,
Her head was facing magnetic north
And her feet were pointing south,
Her lips were black as the weirdest Goth
And her cheeks were pale and white,
I managed to get her breathing then
But something wasn't right.

She stared at me with her purple eyes
That before, I'm sure were blue,

And lightning sparked in her retina
As she said, 'Thank God for you!'
She wouldn't go to the hospital,
She staggered back to the car,
And said, 'I'm needing a drink, for sure,
Let's find the nearest bar.'

I took her home in an hour or two
And I put her straight to bed,
She said her stomach was rumbling,
There was lightning in her head,
She slept right though to the early hours
And got up before the dawn,
She stood and stared out the window, then,
'I think I've just been born!'

I heard her go to the kitchen then,
Where she said that coffee called,
Then heard the clatter of cutlery
Went down, and was appalled,
For spoons were sliding along the bench
Each time that she waved her hand,
When the coffee pot spun off its top
She said, 'Now ain't this grand!'

'That lightning's made you magnetic,
I don't know what we're going to do,
For all things loose and metallic now
Are turning to follow you.'
I called a friend who was trained in this,
I thought he was more than wise,
'We'll have to construct a Growler, but
It has to be oversize.'

A Growler's simply an A/C coil
That you drop the magnet in,
It only takes a moment or so
To reverse that power within,
It took him over a day to make,
We stood her inside the coil,
I turned my back when he switched it on
And listened to Midnight Oil.

She blew every circuit in that thing
The coil was glowing red,
And lightning was flashing in her eyes
While thunder burst from her head,
She was twice as strong as she'd been before
And everything metal stuck,
We peeled the spanners off at the door
While Helen just ran amuck.

She went to live on a mountain top
Away from the bustle and pace
She said she couldn't come back to me,
Nor even the human race,
There's nothing metallic up there, she says
So lives up close to the sky,
And hopes to be struck by lightning, once,
She says that it's worth a try!

A Letter from Bedlam

They have me chained in this noisome cell
With its smells, its moans and shrieks,
No wonder they call it Bedlam for
I haven't slept in weeks,
They brought me here from the Bridewell,
For they said I was raving mad,
I swapped a cell for a place in hell
And the food in here is bad.

We're chained and beaten by loutish guards
And starved and purged as well,
Unless we vomit and take the cure
They bleed us in the cell,
I see the others who beat their heads
On posts, and the old stone wall,
Hoping to join the peaceful dead
When they have no blood at all.

The rats will nibble at hands and feet
If we sleep too deep, and soon
You'll hear the patter as hundreds scatter
About the cell in the gloom,
There are chains and shackles around my neck
My waist and my ankles too,
The only part is my beating heart
Where they can't chain me from you.

I live with the shrieks and moans and groans
Of the most demented souls,
The prostitutes in their open cells
Who squat on the sewer holes,

A guard says he will take care of you
And I know just what he means,
Be true my love, he'll take hold of you
And I know the man's unclean.

I should have minded my temper when
I was walking in the yard,
Was cursed by the devil's tempter, then
I hit the Bridewell guard,
I hang on tight to my sanity
For I never scream or shout,
And hope for the governor's lenity
That they come and let me out.

The visitors come and they poke their fun
At the lunatics in here,
They hold their noses and spit at us
And they make their feelings clear,
We're only scum in the world they're from
If the fools could only see,
That our putrid state could be their fate
In seventeen sixty-three!

The Misunderstanding

Some say that life is a mystery
That we have to pay our dues,
It's written in every history
Marked out by a series of clues.
So it was when I saw her sally forth
With that lost refrain of us,
Older now, but a constant muse
As we caught the self-same bus.

I hadn't seen her in twenty years,
Her temples were going grey,
She'd gained a little in weight, I thought,
Since she'd stormed on out that day.
She didn't see me at first, I know.
Or she might have raised a fuss,
But I sat beside her, anyway
On the rearmost seat of the bus.

She huddled up in the corner when
She saw just who it was,
I couldn't get her to speak at first
And I felt a sense of loss.
'Fancy seeing you now, out here,'
I began, 'it's been a while.'
Could I detect the hint of a tear?
There was no sign of a smile.

'It's been forever,' she said at last,
'And I'll thank you now to go,
I have no need of ghosts from the past
In the life I've come to know.'
I heard my voice, it broke in my throat
As I tried to suppress a sigh,
'I have no wish to alarm you now,
But I thought to ask you, Why?'

'Why did you leave that sunny day
In that terrible month of June,
You said you were going to make me pay
When I came back into the room.'
'You know full well that I had to leave
When that woman knocked at the door,

That painted Jade, that Jezebel,
That blonde, unspeakable whore!'

My jaw dropped open in bleak surprise,
I struggled with grim intent,
I couldn't think for the life of me,
Or remember who she meant.
'There was no woman, as I recall
Though you always thought there was,
Your paranoia was there on call…
Did you mean my region's boss?'

The mist was beginning to clear away
From that mystery, lost in time,
'My god, she called to discuss our costs,
Did you think that she was mine?'
She stared at me and her face went pale
As the truth came home to bite,
'I sat and waited for months, when you
Didn't come home that night!'

A tear now flowed down her pale white cheek
And she turned her face from me,
She stared on out of the window at
Some vagrant, passing tree.
'I always loved you alone,' I said,
But she'd never brooked delays,
We both got off at the same bus stop,
And went our separate ways.

Crow Fly-Over Night

Bring all the kids on home from school
And gather the pets in tight,
Send out and warn the village fool
For it's Crow Fly-Over Night.
Stable the horse, bring in the geese,
Shut up the chicken run,
We can't rely on the local police
So load me a scatter gun.

Shut the windows in both the Utes,
Drive the car in the shed,
Lay out my anti-vermin boots
And a helmet to cover my head.
Lock the shutters and pull the blinds,
We don't want to show a light,
Set the locks on the window-winds
For it's Crow Fly-Over Night.

Then watch for the man in the hood and cape
As he drifts in, under the Moon,
If I sight him well, then he won't escape,
Not like in the month of June.
He brings his carrion in to feed
In a flutter of feathered blight,
If he's not dead yet, then he will be soon
For it's Crow Fly-Over Night.

And the widow Raines in her mourning dress
Has been seen to stray, she roams,
She scatters seed in the wilderness
But the Crows will pick her bones.

At dusk they come in an evil cloud
But with not a single caw,
Then settle over the land, and loud
Announce the word is 'war'.

So hide the children beneath their beds
And bar each door in place,
Block up the chimney flu with lead
And call your sister, Grace,
If she doesn't come before the Crows
She'll find the door locked tight,
And then she'll know what the Devil knows,
It's Crow Fly-Over Night!

The Burial

The sky was dark, it was overcast
When the hearse rolled into town,
The people stopped in its passing,
And stood, with their eyes cast down,
Four black, high stepping, friesian mares
Stepped proud, ahead of the hearse,
While a man was following close behind
But sat on his horse, reversed.

His wrists were bound with a length of twine
Were tethered behind his back,
His eyes were well blindfolded,
Under his black top hat,
His leather boots had glistened and shone
And they rode right up to the knee,
There was something about his stately mien
That said, 'Aristocracy'.

The horses were decked with ostrich plumes
Fine harness and plaited tails,
The coach shellacked in a shiny black
And fitted with silver rails,
The coffin lay on a satin tray
In the hearse, was covered in lace,
Inscribed with scrolls from the honour rolls
Of a noble house, disgraced.

And far at the rear of the slow cortege
Was a line of women in black,
Carrying jewellery fashioned in jet
As black as the coach shellac.
There wasn't a tear amongst them all
Nor a smile for the ruined man,
The blindfold merciful, like a pall
In front of his ruined clan.

The hearse rolled into the cemetery
And stopped by the gallows tree,
A footman took off his blindfold then,
'I hope that's not meant for me!'
They dragged the coffin out of the hearse
And the man looked once, then twice,
'I'm not your common old peasant, sir,
I'm the Lord of Mecklen Weiss.'

They dragged him bodily off his horse
And lifted the coffin lid,
'You're the Lord of six square feet of earth,
And the Lord of all you did!'
They thrust him into the coffin then
Encased his struggling form,

'He'll have some time to consider now
It were best he'd never been born!'

They lowered the coffin into the ground
To the sound of shrieks and cries,
But not one woman who watched it fall
Had a need to dry her eyes.
They say that some heard muffled cries
At that grave for a week or more,
But then, the peasantry always lies
For they hold the Lords in awe.

Bells & Motley

The Jester put on his cap and bells
For the final time, we're told,
The Queen was set to replace him for
She said he was far too old,
'He doesn't amuse me like he did
Before, when we all were young,
Should I dispense with his services,
Or command the Jester hung?'

Her courtiers were gathered around,
They wanted to please the Queen,
Lord Chalmers said, 'Suspend by his feet!'
Then Darnley: 'No! By his spleen!'
'Tar and Feather him,' said Bottolph,
'And run him around the town,
Then tether him to a stake, and light
Him up, in the palace grounds.'

The Queen thought that was hilarious,
And clapped and cried in her mirth,
'By Jove, we'll have us some jesting yet,
We'll bring him on down to earth!'
'He's sure to appreciate the jest
For he won't deny your fun,'
The Chancellor of the Exchequer said,
'We'll gather in everyone.'

While the Jester sat in his lonely room
In a dark and evil tower,
He knew that he would be summoned soon
But he didn't know the hour.
He wondered if she might knight him then
For his services to the crown,
Or grant him a fabulous pension for
The years that he'd played the clown?

For Jesters, they are but mortal men
Aside from their clownish role,
Down under bells and motley lives
A far from perfect soul,
The jesting covers a beating heart
That is rarely ever seen,
And his was filled with a lifetime love
For Her Majesty, the Queen.

He'd loved her since, as a little girl
She'd laughed and played in the grounds,
While he'd leapt out of the bushes there
To her squeals, and laughs and frowns,
He'd always jingled his bells for her,
And carried her in to tea,
When she was sleepy and all laughed out
After playing so happily.

He knew that he'd made more enemies
Than friends, as the years went by,
For jealousy breeds in a court with needs
And the courtiers were sly,
They took it in turns to trip him up
And to hurt, as part of the jest,
But he took new heart at the cruel laughs
By the ones who were not impressed.

He finally stood in front of the Queen
And bowed right down to the floor,
He looked for a smile on her much loved face
But a scowl was all he saw.
'You've come to the end of your usefulness,
A Fool on a bended knee,
Take him outside and string him up,
Upside down from a tree!'

He hung for an hour in misery,
And then they had cut him down,
Tarred and feathered his motley'd form
And beat him around the town.
They wanted to stake and light him up
But the Queen said, 'Let him go.
Give him a crown in a silver cup
For the years he amused me so!'

They cast him out in a farmer's field
And barred him then from the court,
He wept and wailed in his anguish there
For a day and a night, and thought;
The slings and arrows he'd suffered from
Were now brought up with his bile,

And sweet revenge was his ruling theme,
He planned and schemed for a while.

One night he went to the palace yard
And crept down the cellar stair,
He doctored all the barrels of hock
And the fine French flagons there,
Then some time after the palace hunt
He hid in the servants' hall,
And waited til they drank and were drunk
At the Queen's Most Favoured Ball.

Then Bottolph woke in a barrel of tar,
And Chalmers hung by his heels,
While Darnley woke in a quivering fear
In a barrel of snakes and eels,
The Queen awoke in her stately bed
Pinned down by a giant sow,
And wearing the Jester's bells. He said,
'Who is the Jester now?'

Heart Stopper!

He crashed on into our dining room
Like a man convulsed with pain,
And breathless, gasped as he tried to ask,
'What have you done with Jane?'
I stood En Guarde by the mantelpiece
And clutched at a kitchen knife,
'Who are you, and what do you want?
You're talking about my wife!'

He leant exhausted against the wall
And groaned, like a man obsessed,
I thought he could have escaped somewhere
That he might have been possessed.
'I can't believe she's done it again,
She's going against the plan,
I've told her time, and time out of time
To wait for her rightful man.'

'See here,' I said, with a touch of fear,
'She's mine, with never a doubt,
We married a couple of years ago
So I think I'll show you out.'
'I have to stay 'til I see her face
She'll remember when I do,
If you can't stand up to the challenge, then
She never should be with you.'

He'd hit a nerve, and he knew he had
For I'd never been too sure,
For Jane had always been hesitant
When I'd asked for her hand before.
I thought there might have been someone else
Lurking behind her fan,
A former lover, she'd have no other
Now here was this crazy man!

I sat him down in an easy chair
And gave him a shot of Beam,
Then took a double shot for myself,
And stared at him, in a dream.
I tried to imagine her with him
And it shook me, without doubt,
For I could tell that they'd couple well,
Then wished that I'd thrown him out.

Jane came back home from her shopping spree,
Came in through the broken door,
And stood aghast at the pile of glass
He'd smashed there, down on the floor.
The stranger stood, he jumped to his feet
And held out a shaking hand,
'I thought I saw you out in the street,
Don't you know me, I'm your man!'

She held her nerve and she looked at him
As a stranger, far away,
'I seem to recall,' she muttered, 'but…
'All that was another day.'
'Another day in a another time,
The fifth, but never the last,'
He looked at her with his pleading eyes,
Please try to remember the past.'

Then Jane went white as a cotton sheet
And said, 'You couldn't be Paul!
I left you last in the marketplace,
Leaning against a wall.'
'The soldiers came, and took us away,'
He said with the slightest tear,
'They took us behind a barn that day…'
I said, 'What's going on here?'

It was suddenly like I'd disappeared
There were only two in that room,
Their eyes were locked in an act of grace
That I couldn't share in the gloom.
'Of course, it's coming on back to me,
The bed in that cheap hotel,'

She seemed to blush as her eyes cast down,
And my heart had stopped, as well.

'I've had just all I'm about to take,'
I said, 'I want you to go!
And Jane, just tell me for heaven's sake
You continue to love me so.'
The man stood up and he shook her hand
And he said, 'That's really an art.
I didn't think you could act, my dear,
I was wrong, you get the Part!'

Zanzibar!

She lay so pale, under a veil
On the hard mortician's tray,
A tube ran down from her artery
And her blood was seeping away,
I'd never seen her so still and white,
So cold, and her eyes so glazed,
I shook my head when they said, 'She's dead!'
More than a little dazed.

It had only been just a week ago
That I'd gone to call on Jan,
And there, right under the portico
I'd met her sister, Anne.
I'd heard about her before, of course,
The mysterious older Sis,
Who'd travelled far, was in Zanzibar,
Hong Kong and the Middle East.

I'd wondered how she could pay her way
When I heard the awesome tales,
This woman trekking the Russian Steppes
And ending up in Wales.
Now here she was in a Sydney Street
Not a hair was out of place,
Her eyes were shining to greet and meet,
Deep set in her suntanned face.

I must admit that she stirred me then
So I had to drop my eyes,
I'd been with Jan since I don't know when
So I thought it more than wise,
A jealous woman is worse than hell
And I'd rather stick with bliss,
So reached for Jan and I held her hand
As she introduced her Sis.

She'd come to stay for a month, she said,
Then had to be on her way,
She had to meet with a Turkish man
In a market in Cathay,
But Jan was not even curious,
Though the questions crossed my mind,
Most of them would be spurious
But I wondered what I'd find?

What was her line of work, I thought,
How did she make it pay?
Was she some rich man's paid consort
In a Persian alleyway?
Was she smuggling drugs or guns
With secrets tucked in her bra,

Or was she a spy for love, or funds
From a man in Zanzibar?

She settled in to a set routine
In the house, it was absurd,
She always seemed to be normal, not
The hellfire that I'd heard,
We'd sit up late by a blazing grate
Play cards, and drink and rave,
Then Jan went off for her monthly trip,
And she said, 'You two behave!'

She laughed at us as she left, and said
That she'd be back in a week,
It was always some promotional tour
But of what, she wouldn't speak.
For both these sisters were secretive
Tight lipped on the things they'd do,
But when she'd gone, Anne came on strong,
And said, 'I'm looking at you!'

Jan crept back in about midnight, and
She caught us both in bed,
She screamed and ranted about the room,
Went quite right off her head,
She pulled a knife and she went for her,
The startled sister, Anne,
'You've always stolen the one I loved,
And you! You're never my man.'

The body lay on the silver tray
As they walked me in, then out,
Identifying the corpse, they said
So there wasn't any doubt.

They placed me cuffed in a Candy Car
On a charge of Murder One,
While Anne was headed for Zanzibar
As I said goodbye to Jan!

www.ingramcontent.com/pod-product-compliance
Lightning Source LLC
Chambersburg PA
CBHW061654040426
42446CB00010B/1732